Contents

What printing presses yield we think good store
But what is writ by hand we reverence more!

John Donne

What would he have said about the internet?

NETTING YOUR ANCESTORS

Tracing Family History

on the Internet

STUART A. RAYMOND

THE FAMILY HISTORY PARTNERSHIP

Published by
The Family History Partnership
PO Box 502
Bury, Lancashire BL8 9EP

Copyright © Stuart Raymond

ISBN: 978 1 906280 00 0

First published 2007

Printed and bound at The Alden Press
De Havilland Way, Witney, Oxon, OX29 0YG

Preface

Who do you think you are? The question posed by the B.B.C's television programme is encouraging many people to trace their family history. Most turn to the internet to begin their research. The internet is easy to use, it has a huge amount of information, and, increasingly, it is instantly available for use at home. If you want to know more about your family history, all you have to do is to turn the computer on and visit a few websites. It offers a very easy introduction to researching your ancestors.

The internet speeds up the pace of research. It is a particular boon to those who live thousands of miles away from the records they need to consult. It provides an almost instant response. It offers not only an alternative method of research, but also a means of greatly improving the effectiveness of traditional research methods. You will still need to consult books and archives. Much of the information they contain may never appear on the internet. You will still need to make visits to libraries and record offices. But the internet will enable you to be much better prepared for those visits. It will enable you to make much more effective use of books, libraries, and archives.

This book offers an introduction to internet research for family historians. It assumes that you have some familiarity with the internet - that you know what a webpage looks like, and that you are able to use email. It assumes too that you have at least read a good basic introduction to family history. If you have not, a number are suggested on page 17. Chapter 2 identifies a number of web sites offering basic introductions. The information they provide is generally not as detailed as you will find in books.

In this book, web page addresses (U.R.Ls) are printed in bold type. Their titles are given in inverted commas. Some web page addresses are excessively long. Where this is the case, I have explained how to find them from shorter addresses.

A major problem in using a book of this kind is that many of the webpage addresses suggested may be out of date by the time you come to use them. There are various ways of getting round this problem. Some solutions are suggested below, pp. 22-3.

Abbreviations

F.F.H.S. Federation of Family History Societies
I.G.I.   International Genealogical Index
L.D.S.   Latter Day Saints
T.N.A.   The National Archives
U.R.L.   Uniform Resource Locator (i.e. web page
          address)

Acknowledgements

A number of people have made a major contribution to the publication of this book. It was typed by Cynthia Hanson. Richard Ratcliffe and Simon Fowler read the typescript and helped me make it (I hope) more readable. The front cover was designed by Steve Hayes. The fisherman is James Kingdon. Bob Boyd saw the book through the press. I am grateful to all of these individuals for their assistance. I am grateful too the web masters who have given permission for their webpages to be reproduced here.

Stuart A. Raymond

1. *Introduction: The Three Revolutions*

In the last two decades, a revolution has taken place in the way in which human memory is stored, and human thought disseminated. This revolution is based on the technological discoveries and inventions of previous centuries. The discovery of electricity and radio waves, the spread of telecommunications across the entire world, the invention of the telephone, the television, and the computer - all these contributed to the establishment of the internet. It is now possible to store data on a computer in Melbourne, and to access that information via a computer anywhere else in the world, instantly. 'A little history of the World Wide Web' **www.w3.org/History.html** provides a technical outline of how this revolution developed. The principal developments for British genealogists are outlined in Genuki's 'British Isles Genealogy on the Internet: Timeline' **homepages.gold.ac.uk/genuki/timeline**

The internet revolution was the third revolution of its kind, and is dependent on its predecessors. Thousands of years ago, writing was invented. For the first time, it became possible for information to pass between two people without them meeting each other, and without other human intermediary. The use of clay tablets, papyrus, parchment, paper, and writing instruments such as the stylus and the quill, make it possible for us to read the thoughts of people who lived many generations ago. The invention of writing meant that, for the first time, books could be written, records kept, and letters sent. It ceased to be quite as important to memorise information in the head: writing did it for you. The written word was often thought to be much more reliable than the spoken word. Indeed, the written word became so authoritative that it formed the basis of several religions - Hinduism, Judaism, Christianity, Islam. 'Infallible' sacred scriptures are a product of the invention of writing. The desire to read them was a major reason for the spread of literacy in Europe after the Reformation. That desire, however, could only be satisfied as a consequence of another major revolution in the history of recorded memory.

The second major revolution was brought about by the invention of printing. This had been known to the ancient Chinese, but they failed to develop its potential. When Gutenberg brought printing to Europe its use had far-reaching consequences. Its impact continues to spread, even today.

Printing enabled any number of identical copies of the same text to be automatically produced. This at once did away with the intensive labour necessary to produce a single copy of a manuscript book. Manuscript book production had been very expensive. Printing made book production cheap. And it made sure that copies were identical, whereas that could not be said of any handwritten book.

Printed books could be distributed much more widely than manuscript copies. Books ceased to be luxuries that only the privileged few could afford. The Bible could be mass produced. In the mid-sixteenth century a copy was placed in every English church. Even the ploughman at his plough could afford a copy. That alone gave many thousands the incentive to learn to read. Printing also revolutionized bureaucratic procedures. Records could be kept much better by using printed forms. The clergy kept much more accurate and informative marriage registers after the use of printed forms was ordered in 1754. Civil registration and the census depended upon the use of printed forms. Neither of these records could have been compiled without them.

The ripples from these two revolutions are still with us. Indeed, our use of the internet depends upon them. It is impossible to envisage the internet without the alphabet. And computers produce more printing, not less. The age of the paperless office has not yet arrived.

Three revolutions: writing, printing, and the Internet. It is important that we understand and appreciate the relationships between them. Family historians in particular need to be comfortable in handling the different types of documents they produce, i.e. manuscripts, books, and webpages. There are two vital skills required:

- an understanding of how to find information in all three types of document
- an ability to assess the value of the evidence that is found in them.

This book is devoted to an assessment of the strengths and weaknesses of the Internet for family historians. It is particularly important to appreciate that it needs to be used in conjunction with archives, books, and libraries. Their uses are not considered in detail here. For discussion of their importance, reference should be made to the books by Lumas and Raymond listed at the end of this chapter.

It is necessary to begin by emphasising the importance of original sources, which are the subject of chapter 4. They underpin all the activities of the family historian. The majority of original sources are in manuscript, but some, e.g. newspapers, trade directories, are printed. In the last few years, many of the most important original sources have been digitised - especially the census, and the indexes to civil registers. Whilst these can still be consulted in record offices, on microfiche, and often on CD, the easiest way to consult them now is undoubtedly the internet.

A major problem for users of the web is the difficulty of finding information on it. Search engines and internet gateways are the prime means of tracking down particular websites and pages. They are mostly inadequate. You need to understand their peculiarities in order to use them efficiently. This is dealt with at length in chapter 3.

The major advantages which the Internet has over archives and the printed book are:

- ease and speed of access
- currency (although the date of the last update should always be checked)
- the ability to communicate with other researchers instantly
- the low cost of publishing information (much of which might otherwise not be published)

A huge amount of genealogical information is now available on webpages. This includes:

- Basic genealogical guidance
- Sources: digitised images, transcripts, indexes, and detailed guidance on specific topics
- Details of institutions such as libraries, record offices, and family history societies
- General information on the historical and geographical background, including gazetteers
- Lists of surnames currently being researched
- Discussion forums
- Pages relating to particular families

Much of the evidence you need to construct your family tree is online. But you must still verify your evidence in the archives, and use the library.

Further Reading

LUMAS, SUSAN B. *Archives*. Basic facts about ... series. F.F.H.S., 1997.

RAYMOND, STUART A. *Using Libraries: workshops for family historians.* F.F.H.S., 2001.

2. *Family History Research*

The internet is only one of the tools that you need to use in order to trace your family history. You also need to visit libraries and archives, to read books and manuscripts, to interview elderly relatives. A detailed introduction to family history research is beyond the scope of this book. Numerous basic introductory guides are available in bookshops and libraries. A few are listed at the end of this chapter. Books generally provide more information than the many introductory webpages that are available, although the latter may be more up to date. Many changes are currently taking place in the family history world, especially on the internet. It is therefore, always worth checking the last date on which a particular page was updated. This is often given at the foot of the page.

Introductory webpages are provided by a wide range of institutions. Many are listed on the 'General UK Sites' section of 'Cyndis list', at **www.cyndislist.com/genuk.htm**. A wide range are also listed in Chapter 2 of *Family history on the web* (4th ed. F.F.H.S., 2006), which acts as a companion to this book. The B.B.C's 'Family history' pages **www.bbc.co.uk/history/familyhistory**, for example, reflect the wide interest aroused by 'Who do you think you are?' Like many similar pages, the information it provides is fairly brief. Generally, the most reliable pages are provided by institutions such as family history societies, libraries and record offices.

A number of brief guides are available from Genuki, although some of these are now rather dated. These can be accessed via Brian Randall's 'Getting started in Genealogy and Family History' at **www.genuki.org.uk/gs**.

Both the Society of Genealogists, and the Federation of Family History Societies (F.F.H.S.), provide brief introductory pages. The Society of Genealogist's leaflet, 'Starting Genealogy', can be accessed from its Information Leaflets' page at **www.sog.org.uk/leaflets/leaflets.shtml**. This also leads to useful leaflets on a number of other topics. One of these asks 'Has it been done before?' - an important question before you start.

The F.F.H.S's 'First steps in family history' follows a question and answer format. It can be accessed from its 'Help with Research' page at **www.ffhs.org.uk/General/Help**, which again also leads to a number of useful pages on other topics. The pages of other family history societies (see chapter 6) may also be consulted for basic information on genealogical research.

The 'Family Search' website of the Church of Jesus Christ of Latter-Day Saints, at **www.familysearch.org**, has a variety of introductory guides. Its 'England research outline' can be found by clicking on 'search', 'research helps' and 'E', and then scrolling down to the title. It is written for those who intend to use the resources of the Family History Library in Utah, or the Family History Centres which serve as its branch libraries in many parts of the world. This webpage aims to describe 'the contents, use and availability of major genealogical records'. Similar pages cover Wales, Scotland, and Ireland. 'Steve's quick guide to the **www.familysearch.org** website' **members.lycos.co.uk/familyhistory2/fs.htm** offers a detailed discussion of the range of information and resources available. There will be many mentions of 'Family Search' in the following chapters.

Most research in original sources is likely to take place in record offices. Consequently, many of their websites have detailed guides to family history. The most extensive record office website is probably that of The National Archives (formerly the Public Record Office). It may not be the best place to begin researching your family history, but the various guides on its website should be consulted. 'Family History: your guide to resources' is at **www.nationalarchives.gov.uk/familyhistory**, and provides a wide range of information. The National Archives site is discussed in more detail below, pp. 81-5.

Most other record offices (see chapter 6) provide information for family historians on their webpages. Some have detailed guides. A number of examples may be mentioned. Devon Record Office offers a series of leaflets on 'Family History' at **www.devon.gov.uk/index/community/the_county/record_office/family_history_3.htm**. 'Your Somerset family: a guide to tracing your family history in the Somerset Record Office' can be consulted by clicking on 'Guides to research and holdings' at **www.somerset.gov.uk/archives**. Norfolk Record Office has a page on 'Tracing Your Family Tree' at **archives.norfolk.gov.uk/nroleaflets.htm**. It is always worth checking relevant record office sites for any guidance they may offer.

The great advantage that the internet offers is that it is accessible to all, no matter what the distances. It is therefore, not surprising that there are a number of sites offering advice to those searching from overseas. The 'Family search' site mentioned above has this orientation. L.D.S. resources are also described in Mark Howell's page on 'Researching Ancestors from the United Kingdom using the L.D.S. Family History Center's Resources', at **www.oz.net/~markhow/uksearch.htm**. There are a number of other relevant pages. The Society of Genealogists' 'Notes for Americans on tracing their British ancestry' is at **www.sog.org.uk/leaflets/americans.pdf**. Genuki offers a page on 'Researching from abroad' at **www.genuki.org.uk/ab**. The British Isles Family History Society - U.S.A. has much useful information at **www.rootsweb.com/~bifhsusa**. Comprehensive free tutorials for English, Irish and Scottish researchers in North America are available in 'Mother Hubbard's Cupboard' **www.mother-hubbardscupboard.net**. The English tutorial has fifteen chapters on topics such as civil registration, monumental inscriptions and manorial court rolls.

Further Reading
This is just a small selection of the many guides available, easiest first. Herber is the most authoritative.

ANNAL, DAVID. *Easy family history*. National Archives, 2005.
FOWLER, SIMON. *The joys of family history*. Public Record Office, 2001.
RAYMOND, STUART A. *Introducing family history*. F.F.H.S., 2006.
RAYMOND, STUART A. *Tracing your nineteenth century family history*. F.F.H.S., 2005. There is a similar volume on the twentieth century.
HEY, DAVID. *Journeys in family history*. The National Archives, 2004.
HERBER, MARK D. *Ancestral trails: the complete guide to British genealogy and family history*. Rev. ed. Sutton Publishing/Society of Genealogists, 2004.

3. Finding Information on the Web

The internet has billions of pages, and the number is rapidly increasing. It is not, however, well organised. Locating the particular page that is needed is not necessarily easy. The major sites can usually be found quickly, but those created by individuals and small organizations may be difficult to identify. The fact that you cannot find particular information on the web does not necessarily mean it is not there. You may just need to refine your search strategy.

There are various ways to track down information on the web. Search engines and gateways provide the principle methods of searching. The major difference between them is that, whereas search engines index every page they find, gateways are selective. Gateways normally use some form of subject classification. They are likely to indicate the relative importance of a site, and may include general information on particular topics as well. They have already selected the most relevant sites, whereas users of search engines have to undertake the task of selection.

Search engines may produce thousands if not millions of hits. Many will be irrelevant 'false drops'. Some of the latter can be eliminated by more sophisticated searching techniques. It is usually possible to reduce the number of sites found in a search to a reasonable number. In order to do this, you may need to develop your searching skills.

Search Engines

There are well over 1,000 search engines on the web. A number which are likely to be useful for family historians are listed below. Many others are listed on sites such as **www.searchengines.com** and **searchenginewatch.com**. A variety of similar sites can be found by using any search engine. These sites offer lists of search engines, tips on their use, and detailed discussions of their strengths and weaknesses.

A search engine is a database containing an index of webpages. That index is obtained by automatically surfing the web. Some search engines have extremely large indexes. Google currently claims to list no less than eight billion pages. However, no search engine provides a totally comprehensive index to the web. If you are searching for an obscure page it may be necessary to use several engines to find it. Further, the size of an index is not the only criteria for judging the value of a search engine. Its various search features are also important.

Search engines are used by typing word(s) or phrase(s) into their search boxes. This search is then matched against the database and the searcher is presented with the results in a ranked order. The ranking is determined by a variety of factors, which vary between search engines. These include:

- word frequency on the page and the site
- presence of the word(s) in the title or other prominent position
- the frequency with which the page is listed on other web sites
- the number of visitors to the page
- whether the web master has paid for a higher ranking

Some of these may be quite irrelevant to your search. Consequently, the page you need may be well down the list produced by a search. If the list is long, it may be impossible to find it. For example, a search of 'genealogy' on 'Altavista' produces 80,400,000 hits (there will probably be many more by the time you read this). Faced with a number such as this, it is clearly necessary to work out a search strategy that produces far fewer numbers. That is why it is usually important to use the 'advanced' and 'settings' features that can be found on most search engines.

Settings

The 'settings' or 'preferences' boxes on search engines enable the searcher to limit the features being searched, and to specify how results are to be displayed. The choices offered vary between search engines, but some of the commoner limitations offered are:

- language
- country
- date
- the place in the page where the term occurs, e.g. the U.R.L., the title, the text
- the number of results to be displayed
- the format of results displayed

Some search engines offer other features. Live Search offers the ability to determine how you wish results to be ranked. Google enables you to search for pages in particular formats, e.g. Adobe, Acrobat, Microsoft Excel. Users of Altavista can prevent more than two results from the same site appearing in one search.

Your choice of settings will be determined by the nature of your search, and by the speed of your internet connection. If the latter is slow, you will want to limit the number of results displayed to a minimum, and perhaps to reduce the number of elements displayed in results. If it is fast, then the more results displayed, the better. If you are seeking recent information, then you should limit your search by date. An initial search that retrieves too many results can easily be limited by using 'settings'. Whatever the nature of your search, be sure to make yourself aware of the various options available.

Searching

Always use the 'Advanced' function of search engines. Do not be put off using it by the connotations of the word 'advanced'. In this context, it does not mean 'difficult'. Most search engines enable you to combine search terms in a variety of ways. Most will allow you to fill in boxes searching for:

- All of the words (wherever they may happen to be in relationship to each other)
- The exact phrase (where all the words are next to each other)
- Pages with at least one of a number of words

The best results are likely to be found by using a phrase. Phrases are often indicated by inverted commas. Alternatively, most search engines allow you to search by using a 'Boolean expression'. 'Altavista' provides a separate box for this purpose, although the 'operators' can often be used in the search boxes of search engines which don't have separate 'Boolean' boxes.

Boolean searching depends on three 'operators', 'AND', 'OR', and 'NOT'. One of these is placed between two search terms in the search box. These operators must normally be typed in capitals. Their functions are as follows:

- 'AND' or '&' finds pages containing both specified words, e.g. 'Genealogy AND Pyworthy' should lead you to pages relating to Pyworthy which include the word `genealogy'.
- 'OR' or '+' finds pages containing either specified word, and may greatly broaden your search. It is particularly useful when you are searching for different variants of a name, e.g. 'Raymond OR Reymont'
- 'NOT' or '-' excludes particular terms from your search, and may be useful if a word is used with a number of different associations, e.g. 'York NOT New' will exclude results relating to New York.

Some search engines also enable you to search truncated words, or to insert 'wild cards' by using an asterisk. A search for Sm*th*, for example, would find Smith or Smythe.

Finding Missing Pages

Sometimes you will be trying to find a page for which you already have an address. You type the U.R.L. in, but receive the response 'the page cannot be found'. Or perhaps you locate a page on a search engine, but clicking on the entry does not bring the page up. There are three possible explanations for this. The page may be temporarily down whilst maintainance is taking place. Its address may have changed. Or it may have been removed from the web. There are a number of things you can do:

- Wait for a day or two and try again.
- 'Google' **www.google.com**, when it searches the web, stores a copy of each page it visits in its own 'cache'. If you type the U.R.L. into Google's search box, and find it listed, then you should be able to click on 'cache', and see a copy of the webpage as it was when 'Google' last visited.

- Many old webpages are stored on the 'Internet Archive Wayback Machine' **www.waybackmachine.org** (also at **www.archive.org/web/web.php**). Search its database. On this site you can study the way in which a particular page has changed over the last few years.
- if you have the title of the page as well as its U.R.L., you can search for that title via a search engine. If the site has moved, this may reveal its new address. It is sometimes also possible to search for the final portion of a U.R.L. on a search engine. When webmasters move a site to a different domain, they sometimes retain the names of particular pages.

Other Tips

It is important that you get to know the search engines that you use regularly. Experiment with some of the tips offered above, and on the search engines' own help pages. The more you understand the tool that you are using, the better your results will be.

Secondly, do not give up when your initial search does not produce the desired results. Try to work out why. And re-formulate your search, perhaps using a different search engine.

Thirdly, bear in mind that search engines do not search the data in online databases. Search engines will, for example, find the sites which have the civil registration indexes online. But they will not search them for you. You have to use each database's own search box to do that.

Finally, a more detailed 'Guide to Effective Searching of the Internet' can be read at **www.brightplanet.com/ resources/details/searching.html.**. This includes much more information on Boolean searching than can be given here.

Which Search Engine?

Deciding which search engine to use is a matter of personal choice. The size of the index used does matter, but so do the various search techniques and settings offered. Bear in mind that none cover the whole of the web. The beginner will probably want to experiment, although Google is still the most popular. A number of sites listing large numbers of search engines have already been mentioned. A few of the more widely known sites are listed in the box. Some of these have U.K. versions, e.g. **www.altavista.co.uk**, **uk.yahoo.com**. If this is the case, their front pages will give links. There are also

---

Search Engines

- All the Web
  www.alltheweb.com
- AOL Search
  search.aol.com
- Altavista
  www.altavista.com
- Ask
  www.uk.ask.com
- Excite
  www.excite.com
- Google
  www.google.com
- Hotbot
  www.hotbot.com
- Live Search
  www.live.com
- Lycos
  search.lycos.com
- Yahoo
  www.yahoo.com

---

a number of 'meta-search' engines, which search several other search engines at once. Amongst many others, these include:

- All Search Engines
  www.allsearchengines.co.uk
- Dogpile
  www.dogpile.com
- Metacrawler
  www.metacrawler.com

Most of the time you are surfing the web you will be looking for text. You may, however, also need to look for pictures. The web has innumerable photographs of people, houses, memorial inscriptions, maps, and other subjects. These can be searched for on a number of search engines. 'Google Image Search' **images.google.com** is a good example. Several of the sites listed above have similar pages, which are linked to from their front pages. A detailed guide to 'Finding Images on the Web' may be consulted at **www.bu.edu/library/instruction/ findimages/sengines.html**.

Gateways, Portals, Directories

Sites which serve primarily as guides to web resources on par-ticular topics are usually referred to collectively by one of these terms. Some of these sites are simply lists of web sites arranged in a classified order. Others provide more detailed background information.

Computer geeks will be surprised to learn that one of the most popular directories to sites on the web is itself a printed book. *Family history on the web: an internet directory for England and Wales* was conceived long before the present book, but may be used as a companion volume to it, together with the other volumes in the *F.F.H.S. web directories* series. The latter now includes volumes devoted to Ireland,

Scotland, births, marriages and deaths, war memorials, and British history and heritage. They are available at the 'Internet Genealogical Bookshop' **www.stuartraymond.co.uk**.

These printed directories have two major advantages over those which are only available on the web. Firstly, it is possible to see many more items at a glance than can be seen on any computer screen. Hence consultation is much quicker. Secondly, they are properly classified and indexed, which cannot be said of any web-based directory at present. The major disadvantage, of course, is that they can only be updated every two years - and webpages are continually changing their addresses. If you cannot find a page listed in a web directory, then you should follow the advice given on pp. 22-3. The probability is that it can be found. Few genealogical webpages totally disappear from the internet. Half the battle of   finding them is knowing that they exist.

Family history on the web, with its Scottish and Irish companion volumes, provide a detailed and fully classified listing of the major web sites for British genealogy. Unlike most web-based genealogical directories and links pages, entries have been carefully selected by the compiler, rather than being submitted for inclusion by their web-masters. Hence only sites of general value are listed.

When you have gained some experience of using the web, you will find many useful suggestions for developing your internet skills in Peter Christian's book, *The Genealogists internet.* The numerous web sites Christian lists are linked to at **www.spub.co.uk/tgi3/links.php**.

Cyndi's List

The major online directory to genealogical sites is 'Cyndi's List of Genealogy Sites on the Web' **www.cyndislist.com**. This now has no less than 260,000 links. About 1500 are added monthly. Links are arranged into 160 different categories.

There are separate pages for every pre-1974 county in the U.K., and for major regions in other countries. The site is international in scope, but is strongly biased towards North America. Even so, there are links to many thousand British sites.

The 'Main Category Index' offer a detailed listing of links to pages on particular subjects. Each individual page gives a list of 'related categories'. There are four other 'indexes', which offer less information. They include: an alphabetical index, a brief 'no frills' index, a 'topical category' index, and a 'text only category' index. There is also a 'search it' page which enables you to search the whole site for terms which may appear under several categories. Otherwise, there is only limited cross referencing between pages.

Cyndi's List is a vital tool for genealogists, but it is easy to miss relevant entries when searching it. Each entry is only listed once. But frequently entries could be entered under a number of different headings. And there is no cross referencing.

Genuki
'Genuki' **www.genuki.org.uk** is the major genealogical site for the British Isles. Its aim is to serve as a 'virtual reference library' of British and Irish genealogical information. Its links are a major feature of the site. But it also offers a great deal of general information and guidance. Its focus is on primary source material, rather than research in progress or completed. It does not link to purely commercial sites, nor to sites solely concerned with particular families. A detailed guide is provided by David Hawgood's 'Genuki book' **www.hawgood.co.uk/genuki**.

Genuki has two basic strands. Firstly, a number of pages are devoted to general information about researching family history. The front page includes links to pages on:

- Guidance for First Time Users of these Pages
- Getting Started in Genealogy
- Frequently Asked Questions
- Researching UK and Irish Genealogy from Abroad
- World Genealogy Newsgroups and Bulletin Boards
- Upcoming UK & Irish Genealogical Events (Geneva)

The 'Search Genuki Plus' page **www.genuki.org.uk/search/** enables you to search the contents of all Genuki pages for words that may appear on a variety of pages. It also searches a variety of other sites, including family history societies,

Plate 1. Genuki **www.genuki.org.uk**. Your first port of call for U.K. genealogical information.

surname interests lists, and the National Archives site. The entire Genuki site can also, incidentally, be searched by using search engines which permit you to limit your search by the 'domain name' or U.R.L. (although this will not retrieve Genuki pages hosted by other sites).

There are also a number of general links pages, listed in the box, which are useful for topics dealt with in subsequent chapters of this book.

Genuki Links Pages
- United Kingdom & Ireland Societies
  www.genuki.org.uk/big/Societies.html
- Genealogy Mailing Lists
  www.genuki.org.uk/indexes/MailingLists.html
- Surname Lists
  www.genuki.org.uk/indexes/SurnamesLists.html

The second important feature of Genuki is the heirarchy of geographically organised pages. The general pages at each level of the heirarchy provides much useful information relating to the whole of the area covered. In some instances, there are separate pages devoted to particular topics for that area. The general pages also link to all the pages in the heirarchy immediately below. There are four levels in the heirarchy: the British Isles as a whole, the individual countries and crown dependencies, the pre-1974 counties, and towns & parishes. Hence each country page has links to all its county pages. Each county page links to its parish pages.

Within this heirarchy, there has been an attempt to create a uniform range of subject headings at each level, not always successfully. The extent and quality of the information provided is heavily dependent on the volunteers who maintain the system. Consequently, some county and parish pages have a considerable amount of information. Others are woefully inadequate, or (for a few parishes) non-existent. The list of subject headings used is American. The terms used are those used in the L.D.S. Family History Library's catalogue. They are shown in the box.

Genuki Subject Headings

- Almanacs
- Archives and Libraries
- Bibliography
- Biography
- Business & Commerce Records
- Cemeteries
- Census
- Chronology
- Church Directories
- Church History
- Church Records
- Civil Registration
- Colonization
- Correctional Institutions
- Court Records
- Description & Travel
- Directories
- Dwellings
- Emigration & Immigration
- Encyclopedias & Dictionaries
- Ethnology
- Folklore
- Gazetteers
- Genealogy
- Guardianship
- Handwriting
- Heraldry
- Historical Geography
- History
- Inventories, Registers, Catalogues
- Jewish History
- Jewish Records Obituaries

- Land & Property
- Language & Languages
- Law and Legislation
- Manors
- Maps
- Medical Records
- Merchant Marine
- Migration, Internal
- Military History
- Military Records
- Minorities
- Names, Geographical
- Names, Personal
- Naturalization & Citizenship
- Newspapers
- Nobility
- Obituaries
- Occupations
- Officials and Employees
- Orphans and Orphanages
- Pensions
- Periodicals
- Politics and Government
- Poorhouses, Poor Law, etc.
- Population
- Postal and Shipping Guides
- Probate Records
- Public Records
- Religion and Religious Life
- Schools
- Social Life and Customs
- Societies
- Statistics
- Taxation
- Town Records
- Visitations, Heraldic
- Voting Registers
- Yearbooks

This list does give a broad indication of the information available on 'Genuki' pages. However, American terms can be misleading. For example, if you are seeking information on monumental inscriptions, you need to look under 'Cemeteries'. For parish registers you must look under 'Church Records'. The latter term is mis-used. It actually covers a wide variety of records, but 'Genuki' maintainers use it almost exclusively as a synonym for parish registers. On occasion, maintainers do not seem to know what a particular subject heading means. Some very curious things appear under 'bibliography', and 'genealogy' is often mis-used.

Of course, not all these subjects appear on every page. Most parish pages, for example, begin with a topographical description from a trade directory, and give basic information on subjects such as 'church records', the census, civil registration, and 'cemeteries'. Sometimes there is more. 'Genuki' has many transcripts and indexes of original sources, especially parish registers and monumental inscriptions. There are some maps of parish boundaries. The county pages also include a variety of indexes to original sources. Many features of 'Genuki' will be referred to in the chapters which follow.

Rootsweb

Rootsweb is not, strictly speaking a 'gateway'. Nevertheless, it deserves a mention here, since it does host a large number of genealogical projects, including 'Genweb' (see below). Its focus is primarily American, but it does have a great deal of British content. Its 'Websites: United Kingdom & Ireland' page **www.rootsweb.com/~websites/international/uk.html** lists many important source databases. The 'World Connect' pedigree project is based here. So are innumerable mailing lists and newsgroups (see chapter 9).

Family Records

The 'Family Records' portal **www.familyrecords.gov.uk** gives access to the major government archives for genealogists. It is run by a consortium of The National Archives, the General Register Office, the Family Records Centre, A2A, the General Register Office for Scotland, the National Library of Wales, the Commonwealth War Graves Commission, the National Archives of Scotland, the Public Record Office of Northern Ireland, the Imperial War Museum, the Scottish Archive Network, and the British Library's India Office collection. Its 'partners' page gives basic infomation about each partner, with links to their webpages. Its 'topics' and 'guides' pages provide very basic advice on how to begin, and on some of the major sources held by the partners. This site also serves as the webpage of the Family Records Centre.

Other Sites

'Cyndi's List' and 'Genuki' are the two major gateway sites for British genealogists. There are, however, a range of smaller sites which are also useful. Many are listed in *Family history on the web*. This volume also lists the numerous county pages which are the first places you should check for local information. Three other sites may be mentioned here.

The 'British Isles Genweb Project' **www.britishislesgenweb.org** has a geographical structure similar to that of 'Genuki', although it does not have parish pages. It is part of the much wider 'World Gen Web Project' **worldgenweb.org**, which has similar pages for most other countries. The county pages are the most useful feature of this site. Their content is not uniform, and some offer more information and advice than others. They are predominantly links pages. Some of their links duplicate those on 'Genuki' county pages, but this is not always the case. Unlike 'Genuki', there are links to some useful commercial sites, and also to a few home pages for particular families.

'UK Genealogy' **www.ukgenealogy.co.uk** is primarily a directory of links. From its front page it is possible to visit pages for England, Scotland, Wales, Ireland, surname lists, look-up exchanges, mailing lists and societies. Pages listing sources of information and advice on census returns, probate records, gazetteers, emigration, and civil registration are also available. The country pages link to pages for each county, which list useful addresses and local web-sites. Many of the latter are useful commercial sites.

'Genealogy Links Net' **www.genealogylinks.net** is an international directory of genealogical web-pages. It has 6,000 links on its UK pages. Its county pages are a good place to check for transcripts and indexes of original sources.

Further Reading

CHRISTIAN, PETER. *The genealogist's internet.* 3rd ed. The National Archives, 2005.

RAYMOND, STUART A. *Family history on the web: an internet directory for England and Wales.* 4th ed. F.F.H.S., 2006.

RAYMOND, STUART A. *Scottish family history on the web.* 2nd ed. F.F.H.S., 2005.

RAYMOND, STUART A. *Irish family history on the web.* 2nd ed. F.F.H.S., 2004.

4. Sources

The prime purpose of using the internet for genealogical research is to locate the sources needed to fill in the details of your family's history. It is likely that you will need to begin by checking civil registers, census returns, and other sources which provide evidence of family relationships. A wide variety of sources - trade directories, poll books, poor law records - may enable you to locate ancestors in time and place.

Many digitised images of the original sources that you need are now available on the web, including, for example, census returns, civil registration indexes, some wills, numerous trade directories. There are also numerous transcripts and indexes of original sources, especially parish registers and monumental inscriptions. These resources, and especially digitised censuses and civil registration indexes, make it much easier to undertake family history research.

Family historians must always carefully evaluate the value of internet evidence. It is vital that you try to determine the accuracy of the sources that you use. Even original sources such as census schedules and civil registers are not totally accurate. Their compilers were just as liable to make mistakes as we are. The introductory guides listed at the end of chapter 2 provide valuable advice on how to assess their accuracy.

The vast majority of sources on the web have been copied. The method of copying used is an important factor in determining the accuracy of the copy. The most reliable sources on the web are digitised images of original sources. The digitisation process leaves little room for human error. Websites with digitised images, such as the various census sites listed on p.48, can generally be relied on to provide exact copies of the sources they copy, without the need for further checking.

The indexes on sites with digitised images are usually fairly reliable. However, if the entry you seek does not appear, you should check the digitised images themselves. Mistakes are made by indexers. If you find an error you should report it to the webmaster, so that it can be corrected.

Other evidence on the web is much more liable to human error. The internet offers a highly efficient means for creating and storing indexes and transcripts of original sources. Data entry is not, however, always as accurate as it could be. Some transcribers and indexers produce reliable data. But others do not. The possibilities for errors in copying are legion. Frequently, transcribers and indexers work from microfilm, rather than directly from original documents. Original sources such as parish registers and wills are not always easy to read. If they are on microfilm the difficulty is increased. Some transcriptions and indexes will have been independently checked against the original sources, but this procedure is not invariably followed. Few indexes take into account the probability that the indexer has had to undertake some guess-work. Failure to find a particular entry in an index does not necessarily justify a negative conclusion.

Transcripts and indexes of original sources should always be subjected to critical scrutiny before their evidence is fully accepted. The websites of institutions such as record offices and family history societies are more likely to provide accurate data than sites created by private individuals. Institutions have the resources to check data entry more carefully than is possible for the private individual.

It is also important to appreciate the difference between a transcript and an index. These two terms are frequently confused by family historians, especially on the internet. A transcript should be an exact copy of the original document, letter by letter, word by word. An index is a list of terms in that document (for genealogists, usually surnames) indicating where they can be found. If you find these two words confused on a webpage, your suspicions as to the accuracy of the index or transcript should be aroused. The purpose of an index is to enable you to locate the information required in the original source. It is not intended to be evidence in its own right.

Transcripts are generally more useful than indexes. A transcript should reveal exactly what was written in the original document. It will also record what was written immediately before the particular entry you are interested in, and what followed. The context in which a particular entry appears may be important, and is worth checking. An index entry will simply direct you to the entry, without providing any of this information directly.

Your own web browser is likely to be able to perform the function of an index. Its search facility will enable you to search webpages for particular terms, such as surnames, instantly. This is likely to be useful when web pages have a substantial amount of text.

Digitised images of printed books are frequently found on the web. These include numerous transcripts and indexes of original sources. For example, the numerous registers published in *Phillimore's parish registers* series at the beginning of the twentieth century are increasingly becoming available (on a variety of different sites). This is a welcome development. The evidential value of these pages is not, however, as great as digitised images taken directly from original sources. Printed transcripts and indexes need just as much checking as other sources on the internet. Some editors of the

Phillimore series provided meticulous transcripts; others are woeful.

Transcripts and indexes of original sources on the web can be enormously valuable, despite the problems mentioned above. They should never be regarded as holy writ. But they may well point you in the direction of sources which you need to check, and which would be much harder to identify by more traditional means of research.

Databases

The number of databases online is rapidly increasing. New data is being continually added. It should be noted that databases cannot be searched using the search engines discussed in chapter 2. Searches must be made from the front pages of the databases themselves. There is one exception to this rule. 'Surname Navigator' **www.surnamenavigator.org** permits searches to be made on a range of different databases at the same time. Searches can be made on ten databases for England, nine for Ireland, ten for Scotland, and eight for Wales. Click on 'select country' to begin.

There are a number of major collections of databases. A few are free, but most impose a charge. The front pages of some commercial web sites include a lot of hype about the importance of the information offered, but do not tell you what they are charging for use of their databases. In some instances, it is difficult to discover how much their use will cost until you have identified the particular image that you wish to download. There may be a fee for each download. Alternatively, you may be invited to pay a subscription for a specified period. An attempt has been made below to indicate the fee structure of each web site discussed. Fees may, of course, change without warning.

Another problem you may be faced with is the quality of digitised images supplied. It is difficult to obtain a good image from a document that is faded, damaged, or badly written. Many digitised documents have these characteristics. Occasionally, images may be virtually unreadable. If this happens, bear in mind that two of the major sources - the civil registers and the census - have been digitised for a number of different databases. If an image from one database is unreadable, check whether it is available on other databases.

Many substantial databases are mentioned in the discussion of particular sources below. Some websites include a variety of different databases. These are mostly commercial. They include:

- Find My Past
  www.findmypast.com

This site offers images of the civil register indexes, and of various censuses. A number of overseas and armed forces registers of births marriages and deaths are held. The published list of *Soldiers died in the Great War* may be searched. Divorce records 1858-62 and 1874-1903, passport applications 1851-1903, an index of death duty registers 1796-1903, and a variety of professional and military lists are also on this site. Work is at present in progress on digitising outward passenger lists of the Board of Trade for 1890-1960.

Payment may be made online. Alternatively, vouchers may be purchased from a variety of outlets. A £5 voucher gives you 50 units, which entitles you to 50 views. Higher priced vouchers purchase cheaper units.

- 192.com
  www.192.com/genealogy

This site is primarily concerned with locating people alive today. However, its genealogy page does have the indexes to civil registers, 1837-2003, and the census for 1861. It also has recent electoral registers. Credits can be purchased online.

- Ancestry
www.ancestry.com

This is another commercial site. It has several hundred databases. A number of important census and civil registration databases are included. 'Ancestry' also includes indexes to parish registers, churchwardens accounts, trade directories, wills, biographical dictionaries, and many other sources. A full list can be seen by clicking 'all databases'. You should check this first before using Ancestry's search box. Otherwise you will not know what you are searching.

Payment is by subscription. A full year's subscription to 'Ancestry' costs £69.95 at the time of writing. Alternatively, you can purchase ten views for £4.95. UK customers should subscribe at **www.ancestry.co.uk**, where payment can be made in sterling. The main home page gives details of US prices. Many users experiences of using Ancestry can be read at 'Exploring Ancestry Dot Com and Co UK' **ancestry.blogspot.com**.

- British Origins
www.britishorigins.com

This is a commercial site established in conjunction with the Society of Genealogists, who provide the data. It includes the 1841 and 1871 censuses (not yet completed), Boyds Marriage Index, various indexes to wills, apprenticeship records, and a number of other databases. For 'Irish Origins', its Irish sister site, see below, p.123. Subscriptions entitling you to unlimited searching can be purchased for 72 hours, a month, three months, or one year. Members of the Society of Genealogists are entitled to one free 72 hour session per quarter, plus a 20% discount on orders for hard copies.

- Documents Online
  www.nationalarchives.go.uk/documentsonline

`Documents Online' offers a range of digitised images from the collections of The National Archives. For family historians, there are a number of major databases. Over 1,000,000 pre-1834 wills from the Prerogative Court of Canterbury are available here. The death duty registers, 1796-1811, provide information from about 66,000 further wills. There are also various records of the armed forces. There is a flat charge of £3.50 for every image downloaded.

- Family History Online
  www.familyhistoryonline.co.uk

This site was established by the Federation of Family History Societies in order to host databases created by member societies. It has a very wide range of databases. At the date of writing there were a total of 62,000,000 entries in all of the databases combined, and more are continually being added. Predominantly, the databases are indexes of parish registers, the census and monumental inscriptions. A number of extracts from the *National burial index* are included. A variety of other topics are covered less extensively, for example, settlement certificates, marriage bonds and allegations, Quarter Sessions, wills, convict arrivals in Australia. Access to the 1881 census transcript and index is also offered.

The cost of a search on 'Family History Online' is only a few pence. This can be paid for by purchasing credit online, or by obtaining pre-payment vouchers, which are available from many family history societies. At the time of writing, the future of this site is uncertain.

Plate 2. The Genealogist www.thegenealogist.co.uk has the civil registers and many census transcripts.

> - The Genealogist
>   **www.thegenealogist.co.uk**

'The Genealogist' is run by the well known CD publisher, S & N Genealogy. This site offers the indexes to civil registers (via its sister site at **www.bmdindex.co.uk**) and a range of census indexes and transcripts. It has also digitised a number of printed parish registers (including some of the *Phillimore parish registers* series). Various subscription options are available, costing from £5 per month.

> - British History Online
>   **www.british-history.ac.uk**

'British History Online' was established by the Institute of Historical Research in conjunction with the History of

Parliament Trust, and is free. It is primarily aimed at academic historians. Nevertheless, it has many databases which could be of use to the family historian. It has digitised numerous record publications for London. These include, for example, several volumes of seventeenth century tax lists, and many volumes of municipal records. The 'Historical gazetteer of London before the Great Fire' details the histories of all properties in Cheapside from the twelfth to the seventeenth centuries. There is a database of 'Physicians and Irregular Medical Practitioners in London, 1550-1640', and a biographical record of 'The Rulers of London, 1660-1689'. No less than 52 databases relate to London. For the rest of the country, the site has the texts of many volumes in the *Victoria County History* series. These provide authoritative accounts of the histories of many parishes throughout England, and are essential background reading for the family historian. So are the 1:10,560 scale maps of the Ordnance Survey published between 1844 and 1899. Full lists of senior diocesan clergy for many dioceses are provided from the published *Fasti ecclesiae Anglicanae,* 1066-1857.

Civil Registration

The civil registers constitute the single most important source of genealogical information for the period since they began in 1837. They record the births, marriages and deaths of the great majority of our nineteenth and twentieth century ancestors, giving, for example, the names of babies' parents, details of marriage partners and their parents, and ages at death - all essential information in tracing ancestors.

There are numerous webpages offering information and advice on civil registration. Genuki's 'Civil registration in England and Wales' **www.genuki.org.uk/big/eng/civreg** provides useful information on how to go about obtaining certificates of births, marriages and deaths. Some of the problems that may be encountered in searching are discussed in 'Barbara's Registration Web Page' **home.clara.net/dixons/Certificates/indexbd.htm**. Many similar sites are listed in *Family history on the web*, and, more fully, in *Births, marriages and deaths on the web* (2 vols. 2nd ed. F.F.H.S., 2005). These volumes also list a variety of indexes.

The English and Welsh civil registers (unlike their Scottish equivalents) cannot be consulted directly. In order to find out what information is in them you must purchase certificates of births, marriages and deaths. The historic records are currently being digitised and re-indexed. The new index will presumably become available online in due course (2008?), but there are no plans to make the original registers directly available to the public. You will still have to purchase certificates to obtain the information in them.

National indexes to the civil registers are held by the Family Records Centre **www.familyrecords.gov.uk/frc**. The registers themselves are held by the General Register Office **www.gro.gov.uk**. Certificates may be ordered via its website. The indexes provide the information required to place orders. You need to know the name, the year of registration, the volume number, and the page number.

The historic manuscript and printed indexes to the civil registers have been digitised. They have also been transcribed. Various versions of these indexes are available on the internet. Not all are complete as yet. The post-1984 computerised indexes are also available. Some of these databases have already been mentioned, but the complete list is in the box.

Free access to a transcription of the index is offered by 'Free BMD', although its coverage at present is mainly nineteenth century. 'Ancestry' uses the same database to also offer a free service.

The search mechanisms of all of these sites are not perfect. They may not always find entries which are in the printed index. If a search of one of these sites gives a negative result, it may be worth running the same search on a different site.

Civil Registration Indexes

- 192.com
  www.192.com/Genealogy
- Ancestry
  www.ancestry.co.uk
- BMD Index
  www.bmdindex.co.uk
- Family Relatives
  www.familyrelatives.com
- Find My Past
  www.findmypast.com
- Free BMD
  www.freebmd.org.uk
- The Genealogist
  www.thegenealogist.com

 Archive CD Books

Welcome to FreeBMD.

FreeBMD is an ongoing project, the aim of which is to transcribe the Civil Registration index of births, marriages and deaths for England and Wales, and to provide free Internet access to the transcribed records. It is a part of the FreeUKGEN family, which also includes FreeCEN (Census data) and FreeREG (Parish Registers). To search the records that have so far been transcribed by FreeBMD click on the **Search** button below.

The recording of births, marriages and deaths was started in 1837 and is one of the most significant resources for genealogical research. The transcribing of the records is carried out by teams of dedicated volunteers and contains index information for the period 1837-1983.

PLEASE NOTE: WE HAVE NOT YET TRANSCRIBED THE WHOLE INDEX. A breakdown by event and year can be viewed here

Upgrade to FreeBMD servers

Work to upgrade the existing servers is now complete, and FreeBMD is running on five servers.
In addition, a further four servers have been installed at our datacentre. These servers will be commissioned during November, approximately doubling the capacity of FreeBMD to handle searches.

[Search] [View Images] [Information] [Join FreeBMD] [Transcribers' Page]

The FreeBMD Database was last updated on Thu 12 Oct 2006 and currently contains 123,625,788 distinct records (158,761,747 total records).
On Wed 8 Nov 2006 FreeBMD users did 148,161 searches. (More information)

FreeBMD is kindly sponsored by RootsWeb, www.Ancestry.co.uk and The Bunker.

Plate 3.   Free BMD **www.freebmd.org.uk** offers a free transcript of
the civil registration indexes.

It may also be desirable to check the original index if a particular entry cannot be found. An important feature of both 'FreeBMD' and 'Ancestry' is that they both provide direct access to digitised images of the printed indexes, without having to search for a particular name.

The registers held by the General Register Office are copies of registers compiled by district registrars. The process of copying leaves plenty of room for human error to creep in. Consequently, it is preferable to search the original registers, rather than the copies. These originals are still held by district registrars. There are eighteen indexes to such registers currently online (although they are not necessarily all complete as yet). More indexes can be expected. A gateway to these indexes is available on the 'UK BMD' site **www.ukbmd.org.uk**. They will enable you to order certificates directly from district registrars.

If the district you are interested in is not yet covered by an online index, you may wish to consult off-line indexes held by district registrars. A full listing of their addresses can be found at Genuki's 'English and Welsh Register Offices' **www.genuki.org.uk/big/eng/RegOffice**. Brett Langston's 'Registration Districts in England and Wales (1837-1930)', **www.ukbmd.org.uk/genuki/reg** includes historical information, listing the area covered by each district, and giving details of any changes. He also lists current addresses.

Information from over 90,000 certificates is also available at the 'UK BDM Exchange' **www.ukbdm.org.uk**. This information has been contributed by individual family historians from certificates they have purchased. This site charges a small subscription.

The Census

A census of population has been taken every ten years since 1801, with the exception of 1941. Enumerators' schedules, listing (theoretically) the entire population, survive from 1841, although they are closed to public consultation for 100 years. It is currently possible to see how every household in Britain was constituted at ten year intervals between 1841 and 1901.

It is also possible, from 1851, to identify the parish of birth for every individual listed, and to discover the relationship between the head of each household and its other members. A combination of information from the census with that from civil registers should enable the family historian to reconstruct his family tree for most of the nineteenth century.

Family history on the web lists many webpages offering advice on using the census. A variety of transcripts and indexes are also available.

Beginners are probably best advised to start by visiting the National Archives' research guide, 'Census of England and Wales: read this first' **www.nationalarchives.gov.uk/catalogue/ researchguideindex.asp** (click on title). The Family Records Centre actually holds the census returns. Its 'Census Returns' page **www.familyrecords.gov.uk/frc/research/census- main.htm** includes a 'factsheet' and 'how to use' pages, as well as links to some online census returns. Genuki's 'England and Wales: Census' **www.genuki.org.uk/big/eng/Census.html** has some useful links.

In the last few years, rapid strides have been made towards digitising and indexing all census returns. All censuses from 1841 to 1901 are now available on the internet. A number of sites aim to provide comprehensive coverage of all censuses, but as yet only the Ancestry site is complete. It is reasonable to assume that at least some of the others will be completed within the next year or two. Most of these sites offer both surname indexes and digitised images of census schedules.

National Census Databases

- 192.com
  www.192.com/Genealogy
  1861 only currently available
- Ancestry
  www.ancestry.co.uk
  All censuses available
- British Origins
  www.britishorigins.com
  1841 & 1871; not yet complete
- Find My Past
  www.findmypast.com
  1841, 1861, 1871 & 1891 only available. Addresses
  can be searched for.
- FreeCen: U.K. Census Online project
  freecen.rootsweb.com
  All 19th century censuses, except 1881. Transcript
  rather than digitised images. Very incomplete, but free.
- The Genealogist
  www.thegenealogist.co.uk
  Census transcripts and indexes only, none yet
  complete
- Stepping Stones
  www.stepping-stones.co.uk
  1841-71 only; very incomplete, and no personal name
  indexes

A number of sites offer single censuses only:
- Family Search
  www.familysearch.org
  This site has an index and trancript of the 1881 census.
  It does not have digitised images of the original
  returns. Click on 'Search' and 'Census' and specify the
  census to be searched (there are a number for North
  America). The '1881 British Census Indexes Research
  Guide' can also be found on this site, as can a number
  of other advice pages. Click on 'Search', 'Research
  Helps', 'E' and scroll down to appropriate titles. The
  data on this site was initially published on fiche, which
  is still widely available in libraries. A CD version is
  also available from the 'Family Search' site (click on
  'order/download products' to order the CD).
- Family History Online
  www.familyhistoryonline.co.uk
  The 1881 census transcript and index is also available
  on this site. This is the same database as is available
  from 'Family Search'.
- The 1901 Census for England & Wales
  www.1901censusonline.com
  This site can be searched by address or occupation, as
  well as by name.

Searching most of these sites requires payment, either pay per view, or (in the case of 'Ancestry') subscription. Free searches, however, are available on 'FreeCen' and 'Family Search'. Both of these sites offer transcripts of the census, rather than digitised images. These are good places to conduct your initial searches. However, if you wish to check their evidence against the original schedules - as you should - then you will need to visit a site that requires payment, or visit a library/record office that has microfilm.

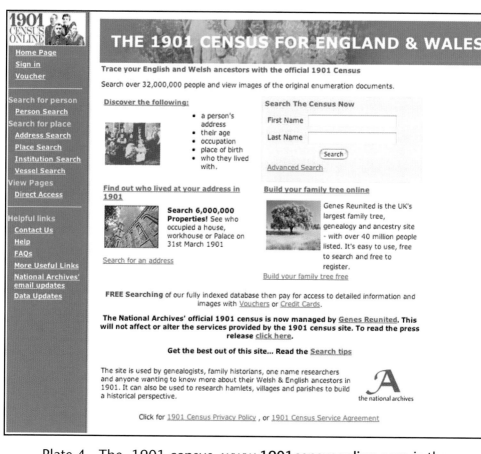

Plate 4. The 1901 census **www.1901censusonline.com** is the most recent that can be searched online.

The websites listed above are all national in scope. There are also numerous pages of census transcripts and indexes covering particular counties and parishes. Many census indexes compiled by family history societies are hosted by 'Family History Online' **www.familyhistoryonline.net**. Others can be found by consulting the pages of 'Genuki' **www.genuki.org.uk**. Cyndi has linked to many census pages on her 'Census Related Sites Worldwide' page at **www.cyndislist.com/census2.htm**. Over 400 pages have links at 'Census Online: England' **www.census-online.com/ links/England**. Many of these sites offer free information.

Digitised images and indexes of the census are also available on CDs from commercial suppliers. Many indexes have been published by family history societies as booklets or microfiche. Webpages listing these will be discussed in chapter 8. A full listing of census websites, together with census copies and indexes in other formats, is currently being prepared in the *Gibson guides* series, to be published by the Federation of Family History Societies.

Parish Registers

Parish registers are the prime sources of genealogical data prior to 1837. After that date, they are eclipsed in importance by civil registration and the census. Nevertheless, they are actually more detailed than in previous centuries, and should not be neglected. They continue to be kept even in the twenty-first century.

Parish registers record the names of those baptised, married, and buried, with dates. Sometimes much more information than this is given. There was no uniformity in the way that entries were made until Hardwicke's Marriage Act 1754 and Rose's Act 1812. Consequently, there is much variation in the information they provide. Furthermore, the handwriting of early registers is not always easy for today's family historian to read, especially when Latin was used. Rod Neep's basic introduction to 'English parish registers', with some guidance on transcribing and indexing them, may be consulted at **www.british-genealogy.com/resources/registers/indexf.htm**.

Unlike the census and civil registration records, parish registers are not held centrally (except in Scotland - see chapter 11), nor is any single organisation responsible for their preservation. Parish clergy had sole responsibility for keeping them. They were required to send transcripts of the entries made in them to their diocesan bishop each year. Most registers - except those still in use - have been deposited in county record offices. Bishops' transcripts may also be found there.

These factors explain why there has so far been very little attempt to digitise English parish registers, or to undertake a comprehensive web-based transcription programme. Medway Archives has digitised many of its registers, and demonstrated what is possible **cityark.medway.gov.uk** (click on 'parish registers online'). It is to be hoped that more record offices will follow their example.

There are numerous transcripts and indexes of parish registers online. Many individuals, and a number of family history societies, have undertaken a great deal of transcribing, indexing and editing. Most of this work has not been co-ordinated in any way. There is a great deal of variation in both the quality and the extent of these webpages. Only a handful of them are of national significance.

The most important index available on the web is the I.G.I. (the International Genealogical Index). This is also available on fiche and CD. The fiche, which is available in many libraries and record offices, was last updated in 1992. The CD version, known as the *British Isles vital records index* was last updated in 1998. The web version is regularly updated, and is on the 'Family Search' website at **www.familysearch.org** (click on 'Search' and 'International Genealogical Index'). The CD may be ordered from the same site (click on 'order/download products').

The I.G.I. is primarily an index to baptisms (or births) and marriages. It is based on two sources. The more reliable information has been extracted from parish registers or other original sources. Much information has also been added by users. There has been no check on user contributed data. It should therefore be treated with caution. The nature of the source from which information is derived is shown on the 'IGI individual record'.

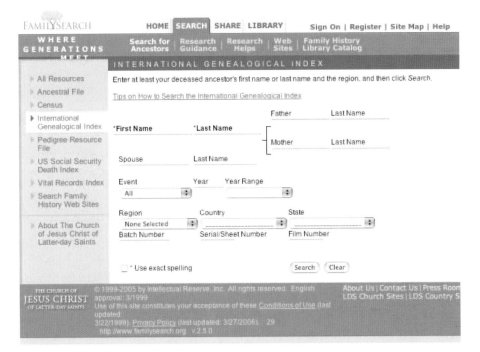

Plate 5. The International Genealogical Index may be consulted on the Family Search website **www.familysearch.org**.

FamilySearch.org (c) 1999-2005 ny intellectual Reserve, Inc.Used by permission

The I.G.I is only an index. It does not include copies of the sources indexed. However, it does give you the information needed to order microfilm copies of sources. Many of these microfilms are copies of original or transcribed registers. They can be borrowed through any of the Latter-Day Saints' Family History Centres, on payment of a small fee. When consulting them, you should always check whether they are filmed from the original registers, or from transcripts. It should be noted that, although a huge number of registers have been micro-filmed by the Latter Day Saints, and indexed in the I.G.I., it is far from being complete.

The I.G.I. does not index burials. In order to fill this gap, the Federation of Family History Societies is compiling the *National burial index for England and Wales,* the second edition of which has been published on four CDs. These CDs contain over 5,400,000 index entries. The entire index is not at present available online. However, many family history societies have placed their contributions to it on the 'Family History Online' website **www.familyhistoryonline.net** A variety of other baptism, marriage, and burial indexes are also available on this site.

'Freereg' **freereg.rootsweb.com** is another attempt to provide a comprehensive online index to parish registers. This site is still in its early stages. Not many registers have yet been indexed. But volunteers are needed to undertake indexing.

Boyd's marriage index is an older major index of parish registers. It was originally created by Percival Boyd between 1925 and 1955, and indexes more than 7,000,000 names from about 4,300 registers, nation-wide. The web version of the index is hosted by 'British Origins' **www.britishorigins.com**. This index is complemented by 'Boyd's London burials index', which indexes 234,000 entries from the Metropolitan area and surrounding counties. Another database on the same site is the 'Marriage Licence Allegations Index, 1694-1850: Vicar-General and Faculty Office'. This indexes 670,000 names, predominantly Londoners. The issue of a licence did not, of course, necessarily mean that the marriage took place. If you find an entry in this database, you should check the parish register too.

'Pallot's Marriage Index for England, 1780-1837' **www.ancestry.com/search/db.aspx?dbid=5967** is another important database. This includes over 1,500,000 entries. Again, many are from the London region, but there are some entries for most counties.

A wide range of other indexes and transcripts of registers are available on the internet. Over 4,000 relevant pages are listed in the two volumes of Raymond's *Births, marriages and deaths on the web* (2nd ed. F.F.H.S., 2005). Some of these pages can also be found through 'Genuki' **www.genuki.org.uk**, but far from all. Most of them have been compiled by private individuals. Some sites cover a wide range of parishes. For example, transcripts of many Somerset registers can be found on the 'Transcriptions' page of 'Roy Parkhouse's Genealogy Site' **www.parkhouse.org.uk/transcr/tcontent.htm**. Others are digitised images of published registers. 'UK Genealogy Archives' **www.uk-genealogy.org.uk/england**, for example, has scanned many transcripts in the *Phillimore parish registers* series.

There are also numerous introductory pages offering local information and advice. Record offices (see chapter 6) frequently have webpages listing the registers they hold and offering general advice. Family history societies sometimes list the whereabouts of local parish registers. They may also offer for sale transcripts or indexes they have published themselves.

Many registers have been published by other organisations. For example, the 'Parish Register Transcription Society' **www.prtsoc.org.uk** has published many registers on CD and fiche for Hampshire, Norfolk, West Sussex, and other counties. 'Parish Register.com' **www.parishregister.com** has an online index to the registers of London's Docklands, and offers a large number of Thames riverside parish registers on CDs. Chapter 8 discusses web-based information on genealogical books, CDs and fiche in more detail.

Monumental Inscriptions

Monumental inscriptions are another valuable source of genealogical data. Tombstones can be found from a very early period. Most, however, were erected in the nineteenth and twentieth centuries. Inscriptions often provide more information than is found in burial registers. Many record entire families rather than just a single individual.

Family history societies and others have transcribed and indexed huge numbers of monumental inscriptions. Much of this work was done before the internet was created, and there are still far more indexes off-line than on. Many societies have published indexes as fiche, booklets, or CDs. Details are usually given on society webpages.

A small but increasing number of societies are placing their indexes on the 'Family History Online' site **www.familyhistoryonline.co.uk**. Some of these are substantial. For example, the 'Cornwall Monumental Inscription Index' has almost 300,000 entries.

A few societies have their own database pages. There are currently 51,223 entries in the Herefordshire Family History Society's index of 'Monumental Inscriptions' **www.rootsweb.com/~ukhfhs/miindex.html**.

The databases mentioned so far are only indexes. They do not necessarily give you all the information on the original memorials, but may abbreviate it.

Many sites include photographs of memorials. These provide more reliable evidence than indexes. However, be warned! Monumental masons did not always carve the correct information on tombstones. Compare it with the information in parish registers if you can.

There are a number of sites which aim at comprehensive coverage of monumental inscriptions. None of these are very substantial at present, although they may grow. It may be worth checking the sites listed in the box on p.57.

Numerous sites provide transcripts and indexes of inscriptions from particular churches and cemeteries. The fullest listing of these is provided by Raymond's *Monumental inscriptions on the web* (F.F.H.S., 2002). The 'Genuki' pages sometimes provide links to them. A few can also be located at Guy Etchell's 'Tombstones & Monumental Inscriptions' page **www.framland.pwp.blueyonder.co.uk**. The majority of these sites have been created by private individuals. The information in them needs to be checked.

War memorials provide a different type of inscription, recording those who lost their lives in the wars (mainly) of the twentieth century. The 'National Inventory of War Memorials' **www.ukniwm.org.uk** aims to create a database listing all memorials in the U.K. Eventually, it is hoped to include the names of all those commemorated. However, this is unlikely to be completed for some years.

A large number of war memorials, from most counties, are recorded at the 'Roll of Honour' site **www.roll-of-honour.com.** This site lists names, and includes many photographs. It also has a 'Medical personnel database', and a 'Boer War compendium of names'.

An alternative resource is the Commonwealth War Graves Commission's 'Debt of Honour Register' **www.cwgc.org**. This is a database of the 1,700,000 men and women of the British Commonwealth who died in the two world wars, and of the 23,000 cemeteries where they are commemorated.

In addition to these major databases, there are numerous sites where photographs or lists of names from war memorials and rolls of honour are recorded. The fullest list of these is Raymond's *War memorials on the web* (2 vols. F.F.H.S., 2003).

Probate Records

Wills and other probate records (inventories, accounts, administration bonds) are invaluable sources of genealogical data. In general, they are the only documents likely to reveal anything concerning the personalities of our ancestors, their religious beliefs, and their attitudes towards other family members. Wills are full of information on relationships. The information they provided was sometimes recorded in death duty registers, so the latter are also worth consulting. The National Archives site has a number of research guides offering useful advice on probate records research. These are listed on its 'Research Guides' page **www.nationalarchives.gov.uk/catalogue/researchguidesindex.asp** and include:

- Probate Records
- Wills before 1858: where to start
- Wills and Death Duty Records after 1858
- Death Duty Records from 1796
- How to Interpret Death Duty Registers

If you are searching for a will post-1858, then you should visit Her Majesty's Courts Service's 'Guide to obtaining copies of probate records' **www.hmcourts-service.gov.uk/cms/1226.htm**. From that date a complete index to wills is held at First Avenue House, 42-49, High Holborn, London, WC1V 6NP. There are plans to place this index online sometime in 2006. District probate registries also have indexes, but these are generally not complete.

Prior to 1858, most wills were proved in ecclesiastical courts. With two major exceptions (see below), most surviving wills are held by county record offices. Their web sites are likely to provide information about them. Few of their holdings are available online, although 130,000 Cheshire wills are indexed on the 'Wills Database Online'

www.cheshire.gov.uk/Recordoffice/Wills/Home.htm. Wills proved in Gloucester 1541-1858 are indexed by Gloucestershire Record Office's 'Genealogical Database' **www.gloucestershire.gov.uk/index.cfm?ArticleID=1335**. A number of other indexes to wills proved in diocesan and archidiaconal courts may be found at **www.familyhistoryonline.org.uk**. Many indexes to wills proved in the ecclesiastical courts were published by the British Record Society in its Index Library. These volumes are widely available in libraries, and are listed at **www.bl.uk/collections/wider/brsindex.html.**

The wills proved in the Prerogative Court of Canterbury (P.C.C.) are held by The National Archives. This was the most important probate court in England. The 'Documents Online'

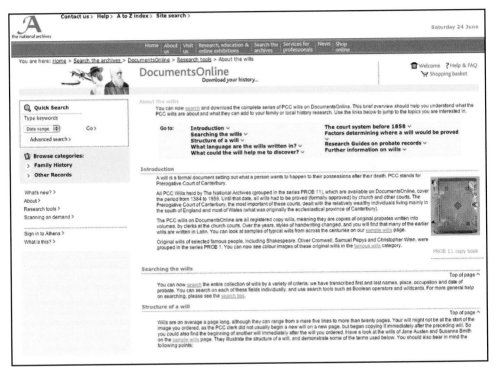

Plate 6.   Documents Online **www.nationalarchives.gov.uk/ documentsonline/wills.asp** has digitised images of over 1,000,000 wills.

webpage **www.nationalarchives.gov.uk/documentsonline/ wills.asp** hosts digitised images of more than 1,000,000 P.C.C. wills proved between 1384 and 1858. These are indexed by name, place, and occupation.

'Documents Online' also has digitised images of the death duty registers, 1796-1811. These are based on wills from a range of probate courts.

The Prerogative Court of York was the major probate court for the Northern Province. Its wills are held by the Borthwick Institute for Archives **www.york.ac.uk/inst/bihr**. With the exception of its medieval wills (see below) no indexes are available on line.

'British Origins' **www.britishorigins.com** has a number of indexes to wills. These include:

- Bank of England Will Extracts Index 1717-1845
- Prerogative Court of Canterbury Wills Index 1750-1800 (incomplete)
- Archdeaconry Court of London Will Index 1700-1807
- York Medieval Probate Index 1267-1500
- York Peculiars Probate Index 1383-1883

A range of other probate sites are linked at 'Medieval source material on the internet: Probate records' **www.medievalgenealogy.org.uk/sources/probate.shtml**. A number of other information pages and smaller indexes are listed in the companion volume, *Family history on the web*.

Trade Directories

Between the late eighteenth century and the mid-twentieth century, innumerable trade directories were published. These provided topographical descriptions of cities, towns, and villages, together with information about local facilities and organisations, listings of private residents and tradesmen, and advertisements. They may enable you to locate particular ancestors in time and place. A useful introduction to this source is provided by 'Using Trade Directories in your Research' **www.genealogyreviews.co.uk/dtippey_trade.htm**.

Original directories may be found in record offices and local studies libraries. A number of institutions have major collections. One of these is held by the University of Leicester. It has created the 'Historical Directories' website **www.historicaldirectories.org**, where digitised versions of over 600 directories, 1750-1919 are available. The site has a powerful search engine, which will take you directly to names on particular pages. It is also possible to browse page by page.

There are many other trade directory sites on the internet. A number are listed in *Family history on the web.* Lists of directories held can frequently be found on the sites of record offices

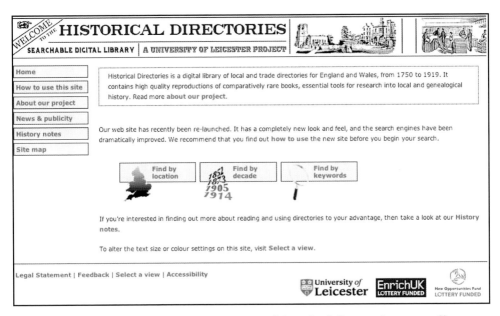

Plate 7. Historical Directories **www.historicaldirectories.org** offers digitised images of hundreds of trade directories, some of which may mention your ancestors.

and libraries (see chapter 6). 'Genuki' has a listing of 'Trade directory holdings in Northern Libraries' **www.genuki.org.uk/big/eng/ncl**. There are also a number of name indexes, as in 'English Trade Directories of the 19th Century' **freepages.genealogy.rootsweb.com/~pobjoyoneill/ tradedir/engtrade.htm**. Some sites provide transcripts or digitised images. For example, directories for Herefordshire and Somerset can be found at 'Genealogy Resources and Documentation' **freepages.genealogy.rootsweb.com/ ~nmfa/genealogy.html**.

There are also numerous brief extracts from directories found on pages dealing with the histories of particular places. Many 'Genuki' parish pages **www.genuki.org.uk** begin with a topographical description taken from a directory. 'Genuki' pages also sometimes link to trade directory pages.

Many trade directories have been re-issued on CD, and on fiche. Chapter 8 provides information on how to identify these. Trade directories may also be located by searching online library catalogues. A useful (but incomplete) listing is provided by the 'County Directories' page **www.british-genealogy.com/ resources/books/directories/index.html**.

Newspapers and Magazines

Newspapers and magazines contain a great deal of useful genealogical information. This includes not just birth, marriage and death announcements, but also obituaries, advertisements for runaway apprentices, accounts of disasters, reports of court cases, and a wide variety of other topics. The main national collection is held by the British Library. Its 'British Library Newspapers' page **www.bl.uk/collections/newspapers.html** includes much useful information, as well as the catalogue of its newspaper collection at Colindale. It has recently commenced its 'Newspapers Digitisation Project' **www.bl.uk/ collections/britishnewspapers1800to1900.html** which will in due course provide internet access to a wide range of digitised newspapers of the nineteenth century.

Another important digitisation project is under way at Oxford University. The 'Internet Library of Early Journals' **www.bodley.ox.ac.uk/ilej** has digitised a number of eighteenth and nineteenth centuries journals. The one most likely to be of value to genealogists is the *Gentleman's magazine* which is currently available for 1731 to 1750.

The government gazettes - the *London Gazette*, the *Belfast Gazette*, and the *Edinburgh Gazette* - have also been digitized for much of the twentieth century at **www.gazettes-online.co.uk**. Use the 'advanced search' facility in order to search the archives (otherwise you will just search recent issues). These gazettes contain a wide range of information - senior appointments in the civil service, armed forces, and the church, awards of medals, notices of bankrupts, lists of persons carrying on certain professions, such as medicine.

The only major national newspaper currently available online is the *Times*. The 'Infotrac' site's 'Times digital archive 1785-1985' has the full text, fully indexed. Details are at **www.galeuk.com/times** for 1785-1985. Chadwyck-Healey's 'Historical Newspapers' site **historynews.chadwyck.com** has the full text available for 1785-1870, together with indexes 1790-1905. Your local public library may have a subscription (which is very expensive) to one of these services. Free access may be possible for library members through its website.

The 'War Times Index' **www.wartimesindex.co.uk** is much less comprehensive, but it is free. It is an index to the names of soldiers mentioned in despatches published in the *Times* in the nineteenth century.

Important 'old technology' is also represented on the web. The 'Newsplan 2000 Project' **news.nlw2k19.userarea.co.uk** is engaged in a major project to microfilm old newspapers for preservation purposes. Its webpage includes an extensive listing of the newspapers which have been filmed.

A variety of other newspaper extracts and indexes are listed in Raymond's *Family history on the web*. Some may also be found through the 'Genuki' pages.

Records of Migration

The British Isles have been a major source of emigrants to North America, Australia, New Zealand, India, and, to a lesser extent, South Africa and many other former British colonies. Tracing these emigrants is a task which may require consultation of records in the countries where they settled. A good place to start would be Genuki's 'United Kingdom and Ireland Emigration and Immigration' page **www.genuki.org.uk/big/ Emigration.html. '**Cyndis List' **www.cyndislist.org** has pages listing websites for most countries in the world. The country pages of 'World Gen Web' **www.worldgenweb.org** may also be useful.

Many records of migration are held by the National Archives. Its leaflet, 'Emigrants' **www.catalogue.nationalarchives.gov.uk/ leaflets/ri2272.htm** is essential reading for the researcher.

Passenger lists are one of the best known sources for tracing the international movements of our ancestors. They are particularly useful for tracing emigrants to North America and Australia. A good introduction is provided by the National Archives research guide 'Passenger Lists' **www.nationalarchives.gov.uk** (click on 'Research, education ...' and 'Research guides', then scroll down to title).

The Board of Trade passenger lists, 1890-1960 are currently being digitised for 'Find my Past' **www.findmypast.com**. It is possible to find thousands of other transcripts of passenger lists on the internet. 'Ships' Passenger Lists: Hugh Reekie's Index of Indexes' **members.allstream.net/~max-com/Ships.html** is a major attempt to keep track of them. A similar links page is provided by 'Passenger Lists on the Internet' **members.aol.com/rprost/passenger.html**. The 'Immigrant Ships Transcribers Guild', **www.immigrantships.net** alone has 6,500 lists online (although not all relate to British shipping).

Cyndi's 'Immigration and Naturalization' page **www.cyndislist.com/immigrat.htm** lists numerous sites dealing with migrants to North America. One of the biggest databases is provided by the 'Ellis Island Foundation' **www.ellisisland.org**. This lists over 22,000,000 names of arrivals in New York (not all British) for 1892-1924. For Canada, the 'Collections Canada' page, 'Moving here: staying here' **www.collectionscanada.ca/immigrants** has a variety of databases of immigrants, as well as much helpful advice.

A variety of sources for emigration to North America held by The (British) National Archives are described in 'American and West Indian Colonies Before 1782' **www.nationalarchives.gov.uk/ catalogue/Leaflets/ri2105.htm**, and 'Emigrants to North America after 1776' **www.nationalarchives.gov.uk/ catalogue/Leaflets/ri2107.htm**

Not all emigrants travelled voluntarily. Australia was founded as a convict settlement, and transported convicts were also a significant group in early American society. Convicts leave a paper trail. Their records can be found in both London, and in the archives of their countries of settlement. For records in The National Archives, consult 'Transportation to America and the West Indies, 1615-1776' **www.nationalarchives.gov.uk/ catalogue/Leaflets/ri2234.htm,** and 'Transportation to Australia 1787-1868' **www.nationalarchives.gov.uk/catalogue/ Leaflets/ri2235.htm.**

A variety of Australian convict databases are linked on the State Library of New South Wales 'Australian resources' page **www.sl.nsw.gov.au/links/fhs/aust.cfm**. A number of other databases for emigrants to Australia are also listed here. These cover topics such as passenger lists and assisted migration.

British migration to India was different in character from migration to North America and Australia. The majority of migrants intended to return home - and many did. The records of the India Office are the prime source of information on them. These are held by the British Library. Details of holdings are given on its 'India Office Records' page, **www.bl.uk/collections/orientaloffice.html**. This includes a separate page on family history research. A useful introduction is also provided by 'Family History in India' **members.ozemail.com.au/~clday**. This site has a number of databases, indexing more than 234,000 names.

Many people moved in the opposite direction, especially in the twentieth century. A detailed guide to sources is provided by The National Archives leaflet 'Immigrants' **www.nationalarchives.gov.uk/catalogue/RdLeaflet.asp?sLeafletID=243**.

Another National Archives leaflet explains in more detail the records of 'Naturalisation and Citizenship: Grants of British Nationality' **www.nationalarchives.gov.uk/catalogue/Rdleaflet.asp?sLeafletID=242.**

The best internet introduction to studying immigrants is 'Moving Here' **www.movinghere.org.uk**. This recounts the history of immigrants in Britain since 1800, and includes digitised images of many inward passenger lists. The National Archives is currently in the process of indexing these lists. The index can be searched at **www.nationalarchives.gov.uk/catalogue/search.asp**.

Poor Law
Many of our ancestors came into contact with Poor Law administration, either as paupers, ratepayers, or overseers. The records are extensive: overseers accounts, settlement examinations, removal orders, and a wide variety of other docu-

ments. A comprehensive introduction to 'The Workhouse' may be found at **www.workhouses.org.uk**. This includes much information on records, including many transcripts of census returns for workhouses. Ross Brett's 'Workhouses' site **www.institutions.org.uk/workhouses/index.html** includes details of all unions. Many record office sites provide useful information on their poor law holdings.

There is little hard Poor Law data online. The 'Index to Paupers in Workhouses 1861' site **www.genuki.org.uk/ big/eng/Paupers** provides a 10% sample of names from a Parliamentary paper which listed the entire workhouse population in that year. The 'West Sussex Poor Law Database 1662-1835' **www.westsussex.gov.uk/ccm/content/ libraries-and-archives/record-office/family-history/ poor-law-database.en** indexes over 6,000 names found primarily in settlement certificates and removal orders.

Most other poor law data on the web concerns particular parishes. For example, there is an index to 'St. Martins in the Field Settlement Examinations' at **www.westminster.gov.uk/ libraries/archives/indexes/sett_intro.cfm**. A list of 'Sturminster Marshall Bastardy Bonds' is at **www.dorset-opc.com/Sturminster/SturminsterMarshall/ SturMarshBastardyBonds.htm**. The 'Parish of Powerstock Overseers of the Poor Rate Books 1756-1757' are at **www.dorset-opc.com/PowerstockFiles/PowerstockOverseers.htm** Many similar pages can be found through the pages of 'Genuki'.

Other Sources

The internet has webpages for a wide variety of other sources. One which stands out is 'The Proceedings of the Old Bailey, London 1674 to 1834' **www.oldbaileyonline.org**, which has the digitised records of 100,000 cases heard in the court. Many similar records may be found in the records of other central courts. These have not been digitised, but The National

Archives site **www.nationalarchives.gov.uk/catalogue/ researchguidesindex.asp** has many helpful leaflets explaining what is available.

Most transcripts and indexes of miscellaneous sources relate to particular parishes and counties. Some parish sites have extensive transcripts from a wide range of sources. Two parish sites in particular stand out:

- Earls Colne, Essex: records of an English village 1375-1854
  www.linux02.lib.cam.ac.uk/earlscolne
- Wirksworth Parish Records 1600-1900
  www.wirksworth.org.uk

Some 'Genuki' parish pages also have extensive transcripts from local records. Extracts from estate and manorial records, tax lists, quarter sessions, muster rolls, tithe records, and a variety of other records can frequently be found.

It is also possible to find many county-wide sources on webpages. A number of examples are worth mentioning:

- The Dorset Coast Digital Archive
  www.dcda.org.uk
  Includes tithe maps and apportionments
- Pollbook of Bedfordshire 1722
  www.rabancourt.co.uk/abacus/p1722h.html
- Genoot Family History Services: Return of Owners of Land 1873: Oxfordshire
  www.genoot.com/eng/oxf/landowners

Many similar sites are listed in Raymond's *Family history on the web*. They can also be found on 'Genuki' pages **www.genuki.org.uk**, or located via the search engines discussed in chapter 3.

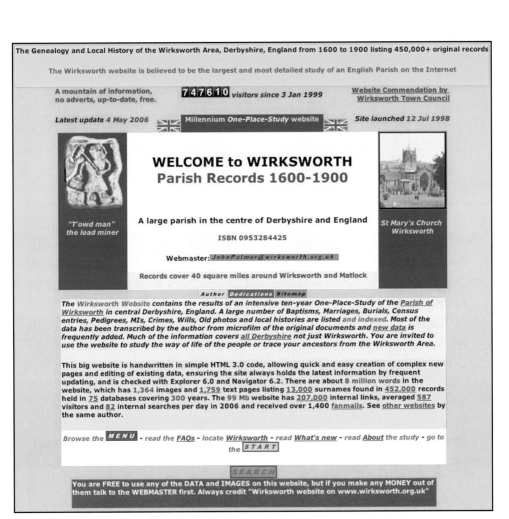

The Genealogy and Local History of the Wirksworth Area, Derbyshire, England from 1600 to 1900 listing 450,000+ original records

The Wirksworth website is believed to be the largest and most detailed study of an English Parish on the Internet

A mountain of information, no adverts, up-to-date, free.

747610 *visitors since 3 Jan 1999*

Website Commendation by Wirksworth Town Council

Latest update 4 May 2006   Millennium *One-Place-Study* website   *Site launched 12 Jul 1998*

WELCOME to WIRKSWORTH
Parish Records 1600-1900

"T'owd man" the lead miner

A large parish in the centre of Derbyshire and England

ISBN 0953284425

St Mary's Church Wirksworth

Webmaster: JohnPalmer@wirksworth.org.uk

Records cover 40 square miles around Wirksworth and Matlock

Author **Dedications** **Sitemap**

The *Wirksworth Website* contains the results of an intensive ten-year One-Place-Study of the *Parish of Wirksworth* in central Derbyshire, England. A large number of Baptisms, Marriages, Burials, Census entries, Pedigrees, MIs, Crimes, Wills, Old photos and local histories are listed *and indexed*. Most of the data has been transcribed by the author from microfilm of the original documents and *new data is* frequently added. Much of the information covers *all Derbyshire* not just Wirksworth. You are invited to use the website to study the way of life of the people or trace your ancestors from the Wirksworth Area.

This big website is handwritten in simple HTML 3.0 code, allowing quick and easy creation of complex new pages and editing of existing data, ensuring the site always holds the latest information by frequent updating, and is checked with Explorer 6.0 and Navigator 6.2. There are about 8 million words in the website, which has 1,364 images and 1,759 text pages listing 13,000 surnames found in 452,000 records held in 75 databases covering 300 years. The 99 Mb website has 207,000 internal links, averaged 587 visitors and 82 internal searches per day in 2006 and received over 1,400 fanmails. See other websites by the same author.

Browse the **MENU** - read the **FAQs** - locate **Wirksworth** - read **What's new** - read **About** the study - go to the **START**

SEARCH

You are FREE to use any of the DATA and IMAGES on this website, but if you make any MONEY out of them talk to the WEBMASTER first. Always credit "Wirksworth website on www.wirksworth.org.uk"

Plate 8. Derbyshire genealogists will find the 'Wirksworth Parish Records site **www.wirksworth.org.uk** an invaluable aid to their research.

5. Tracing Ancestral Occupations

The records of our ancestors' occupations may throw a great deal of light on their lives. Occupations are usually stated in civil registration certificates and census records, and often mentioned in other sources. These clues may enable you to identify more information about them in occupational records.

Many records of employment survive - personnel records, membership lists of professional organizations and trade unions, the archives of regulatory organizations. With a few exceptions, most of this information is not available on the internet. However, a great deal of advice is available. The National Archives 'research guides' page **www.nationalarchives.gov.uk/catalogue/Default.asp**, for example, links to leaflets on:

- Civil servants
- Coastguards
- Customs & Excise Officials and Tax Collectors
- Education: Records of Teachers
- Lawyers: records of Attorneys and Solicitors
- Metropolitan Police (London): Records of Service
- Railways: Staff Records
- Royal Warrant Holders and Household Servants

In addition, there are numerous 'research guides' dealing with the merchant navy and the armed forces. These are important. Most of us had relatives who served in the two world wars. It is likely that all readers of this book will need to consult armed forces records.

An increasing amount of data dealing with the armed forces is becoming available on the internet. The National Archives 'Documents Online' **www.nationalarchives.gov.uk/ documentsonline** has a number of relevant databases. The service records of 500,000 Royal Naval seamen, 1873-1923 provide much useful biographical information. The 5,500,000 index cards for World War I campaign medals may help you to track an ancestor's service in the war. Records of medals issued to World War II merchant seamen are also on this site.

Armed forces records also appear on other web-sites. A number of *Army lists* are available on 'Find my past' **www.findmypast.com**. *Army lists* were (and are) regularly issued, although only a few are online. They list all Army officers. A leaflet issued by the National Archives give full details of 'British Army Lists' **www.nationalarchives.gov.uk/ catalogue/RdLeaflet.asp?sLeafletID=267**.

The records of education have the potential to tell us as much about our ancestors as the records of the army. Unfortunately, this potential has yet to be exploited by webmasters. Virtually all of our late nineteenth and twentieth century forebears had some schooling. Their attendance at school was recorded. Many school registers, log books, and other records survive. A handful of these records are available on the internet. Some are listed on 'Genuki' pages. Others may be discovered using a search engine. Good examples from Worcestershire can be found by clicking on 'Archive' at Quinton Local History Society's site **www.qlhs.org.uk**.

Much more information is becoming available about university students. 'ACAD: A 'Cambridge Alumni Database' **venn.csi.cam.ac.uk/ACAD/index.html** provides information about a projected database of all Cambridge University students, 1200 to 1900. There is no similar project for Oxford students as yet. However, 'Ancestry' does have a database of 'Oxford Men 1880-1892' **www.ancestry.co.uk/search/ db.aspx?dbid=7422**.

Many of our ancestors served an apprenticeship. The National Archives 'research guide' (see above) on 'Apprenticeship Records as Sources for Genealogists' should be consulted for some general guidance on apprenticeship records in its possession. The Guildhall Library's leaflet 'Sources for tracing apprenticeship and membership in City livery companies and related organisations' **www.history.ac.uk/ gh/livdet.html** may also prove useful.

'British Origins' **www.britishorigins.com** has two major apprenticeship databases. Its 'Apprentices of Great Britain 1710-1774' provides abstracts of some 350,000 indenture taken from Inland Revenue tax records (now in the National Archives). 'London Apprentices Abstracts 1442-1850' is a database of London livery company records which identify over 100,000 youths from all over the country who were apprenticed to London masters. It includes details of masters and parents.

A large number of our late-nineteenth and twentieth century ancestors were trade unionists. The Modern Records Centre at the University of Warwick has a large collection of trade union records, which are listed on its website **www2.warwick.ac.uk/services/library/mrc**. The website also has a series of detailed guides to occupations covered by their records. These may be found by clicking on 'Genealogy' and scrolling down. They cover a variety ot trades - bookbinders, miners, seamen, woodworkers, and a number of others.

Employers' personnel records may survive for many of these occupations. As yet, few are available online. One exception to this rule are the 'Railways Staff Registers Online', which can be found on the Cheshire Record Office's site at **www.cheshire.gov.uk/Recordoffice/Railways**. This database is based on the staff registers of four railway companies, and cover much of North-West England.

Personnel records are also included in the 'Hospital Records Database' **www.nationalarchives.gov.uk/hospitalrecords**. This database does not index personal names. Rather, it lists surviving staff records. It also lists patient records. But be warned, these are mostly closed for a century.

The government kept tabs on a number of occupations. For example, between 1850 and 1914 the *Mines Inspectors reports* listed no less than 90,000 miners killed in accidents. Ian Winstanley has included these names in his 'National Database of Mining Deaths in Great Britain', which is a part of the 'Coal Mining Resource Centre' **www.cmhrc.co.uk**.

The 'British Book Trade Index' **www.bbti.bham.ac.uk** is based on a much wider range of evidence, and includes brief biographical details of publishers, booksellers, printers, and allied trades. Many researchers have made contributions to this database.

The professions employed fewer people than the trades, but are well recorded. There are three sites full of useful information on tracing medical ancestors:

- Was Your Ancestor a Doctor? / Alex Glendinning
  users.itl.net/~glen/doctors.html
- Biographical Information: Doctors and Other Professions / British Medical Association
  www.bma.org.uk/ap.nsf/Content/ LIBBiographicalInformation
- Tracing Your Medical Ancestors / Royal College of General Physicians
  www.rcgp.org.uk/default.aspx?page=93

If you are tracing clergy ancestors, begin by reading Lambeth Palace Library's 'Biographical Sources for Anglican Clergy' **www.lambethpalacelibrary.org/holdings/Guides/clergyman.html**. Another useful page is Guildhall Library's leaflet 'Sources for tracing clergy and lay persons' **www.history.ac.uk/gh/clergy.htm**. The library holds the archives of the Diocese of London.

All Church of England clergymen, 1540-1835 will eventually be documented by the 'Clergy of the Church of England Database Project' **www.theclergydatabase.org.uk**. Some 23,000 individuals are listed at the time of writing, but much more remains to be done.

If you are looking for a clergyman active at the end of the nineteenth century, you will probably find him in the published *Clergy List 1896,* which is available at `Find my past' **www.findmypast.com**. The internet also has a lookup service for various editions of *Crockford's clerical directory* (which regularly listed all Anglican clergymen) at **www.rogerco.pwp.blueyonder.co.uk/history/crockfords.htm**. Roger Vaughan, who offers this service, also offers lookups in various public school registers, and in a variety of other reference works.

'Lawyers: Records of Attorneys and Solicitors' **www.nationalarchives.gov.uk/catalogue/RdLeaflet.asp?sLeafletID=98** provides a basic introduction to the records of another ancient profession. Lawyers trained at the Inns of Court. The 'Inner Temple Admissions Register Database' **www.innertemple.org.uk/archive/itad/index.asp**, in addition to providing a list of admissions 1547-1850, also has some useful general advice on tracing members of the profession.

Numerous other occupations were followed by our forefathers. Many are listed in 'Ranks Professions, Occupations and Trades' **homepage.ntlworld.com/hitch/gendocs/trades.html** More archaic occupations are listed in 'A list of

Occupations' **www.rootsweb.com/~usgwkidz/oldjobs.htm**.
A list of other lists is provided at **genealogy.about.com/cs/
oldoccupations**.

This chapter has only covered a small number of occupations, without going into any depth. Many other pages are available on the internet. Some are listed in *Family history on the web*. Others may be found by combining the name of the occupation, and either 'genealogy' or 'history' in a search on one of the search engines discussed in chapter 3.

6. Institutions:
Libraries, Record Offices and Family History Societies

Most institutions of interest to family historians have web-sites. These normally provide contact details, opening hours, admission requirements, details of services provided and infor-mation on their own publications. They often also include cat-alogues, details of collections held, and advice pages. This applies to libraries, record offices and family history societies.

Some of these sites have a great deal more information on them. This chapter examines what can be learnt from them by the family historian. Before you visit any institution holding original documents, you should read 'You and your Record Office: a code of practice for family historians using record offices' **www.ffhs.org.uk/General/Help/Record.htm**.

Libraries
Genealogical research on the internet will be much more effec-tive if it is accompanied by research in books and libraries, as has already been pointed out. A huge amount of genealogical information has been printed. Only a tiny proportion of this information is available on the internet (although digitised images of a few books are available). Furthermore, the printed page is likely to be more accurate than a webpage, since it receives far more scrutiny than the latter before it is printed. Of

course, the evidence books provide still needs to be checked in the archives.

Libraries are store-houses of printed books and journals. They also frequently house microfiche and CDs. Many fiche have been produced by family history societies. Many CDs (usually containing facsimiles of out of print books) have been published commercially. The best way to find out what is available in libraries is to consult relevant bibliographies, and then to check library catalogues on the internet.

There are a wide variety of different types of library: public, university, national, family history society, *etc.* The most useful for family historians are generally the local studies collections maintained in public libraries. Their function is to collect and make available everything published relating to their locality. Their staff are usually experts in finding information relevant to family and local historians.

The 'Familia' website **www.familia.org.uk** offers a summary guide to the genealogical holdings of most British and Irish public libraries. It includes links to many library webpages, which may provide more detailed information. Public library webpages are also listed on the 'UK Public Libraries page'

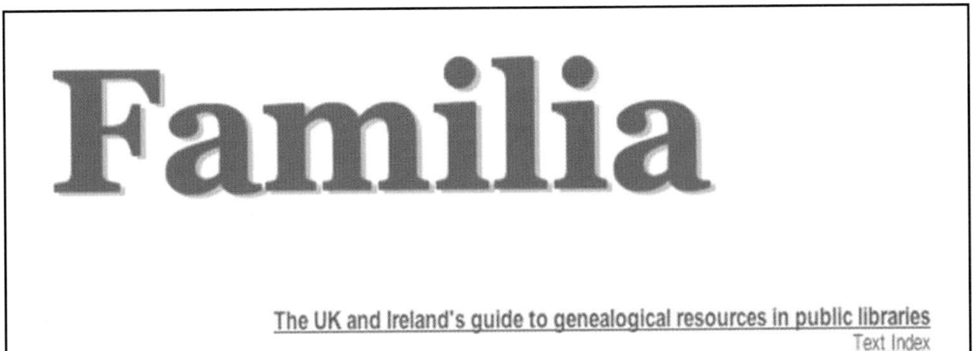

Familia

The UK and Ireland's guide to genealogical resources in public libraries

Text Index

Plate 9. Familia www.familia.org.uk is a directory of genealogical resources in British public libraries.

at **dspace.dial.pipex.com/town/square/ac940/weblibs.html**. Most libraries have a separate webpage or pages for 'local studies' and/or 'family history'. These are listed in *Family history on the web*. Sometimes these pages are extensive. For example, Devon County Council's 'Local Studies' page **www.devon.gov.uk/index/community/libraries/localstudies.htm** links to numerous separate pages. Each collection in the county has its own page. There are also pages dealing with a wide variety of sources and techniques. In addition, the main county catalogue has its own page, as do the separate catalogues of the West Country Studies Library and the Devon and Cornwall Record Society.

Of wider relevance is the web site of London's Guildhall Library **www.cityoflondon.gov.uk** (click on 'a-z', and 'Guildhall Library'). It houses the major collection of London local history, but also holds a wide range of genealogical material covering the whole country. This includes extensive collections of trade directories, poll books, and family history society publications. Its web site includes many helpful leaflets on its holdings, e.g. 'Trade directories and telephone books', 'Brewery history', 'Sources for clock and watchmakers'. Its catalogue is also online, and every family historian is likely to be able to identify relevant material in it.

Reference should also be made to the Latter-Day Saints' Family History Library. This is the largest genealogical library in the world, situated in Salt Lake City, Utah. Most of its holdings are on microfilm, and can be borrowed via its international network of Family History Centres (many of which are in the U.K.). Its catalogue is on the 'Family Search' website **www.familysearch.org**, which also offers extensive 'record guidance' and 'research helps' from its 'Search' page.

Library catalogues are the gateways to their holdings and should be familiar to all family historians. Most public and university libraries now have online catalogues. Gateways to these are listed in the box.

University libraries frequently hold substantial collections of British history, which include much material of interest to local and family historians. Runs of county historical journals and record society publications are frequently held.

A detailed listing of record society publications is provided on the Royal Historical Society's 'Texts and Calendars' page **www.rhs.ac.uk/textsandcals.htm**. This is integrated with the society's bibliography **www.rhs.ac.uk/bibl/bibwel.asp**, which has nearly 400,000 entries listing books and journal articles on British and Irish history.

Bibliographies are invaluable sources of information for family historians. They tell you what information has been published and is available in libraries. Ideally, family historians need to consult county bibliographies, since these are likely to list a wider range of materials. Unfortunately, only a few adequate county bibliographies are available on the web.

> **County Bibliographies on the Web**
> - Lindex: the Lincolnshire Index
>   **www.lincolnshire.gov.uk/section.asp?docId=33190**
> - London's Past Online: a Bibliography of London History
>   **www.history.ac.uk/cmh/lpol**
> - [Staffordshire] Bibliography
>   **www.staffshistory.org.uk/bibliography.htm**
> - Suffolk Bibliography
>   **content.ancestry.com/iexec/?htx=List&dbid=7529**
>   Subscription required
> - Sussex Historians On-Line Bibliography, compiled by John Farrant
>   **www.sussexpast.co.uk/research/histonli.htm**
>   This page has been removed from its server, but may still be consulted at **www.waybackmachine.org**.

The most useful county bibliographies, written specifically for genealogists, are the 'British genealogical library guides', listed at **www.stuartraymond.co.uk/bglg/htm** Bibliographies enable you to identify the particular books or journal articles you need to consult. They can then be located via library catalogues.

Record Offices
Most original sources are found in record offices. 'English Record Offices and Archives on the Web' **www.oz.net/ ~markhow/englishros.htm** lists county record offices, and leads to pages on Scotland and Wales. This page is written specifically for family historians.

The authoritative web-based listing of record offices is the 'Archon Directory' **www.nationalarchives.gov.uk/archon**.

This lists not just county record offices, but also numerous smaller archive repositories, some of which may only hold a few documents. It gives contact details and links to webpages. It also links to individual entries in the 'National Register of Archives' **www.nationalarchives.gov.uk/nra.**

The N.R.A. serves as a listing of collections held by record offices throughout the country. It can be searched online, but its indexes are not designed with the family historian in mind. Its 'personal name' index, for example, only relates to individuals whose papers have been deposited. Nevertheless, it may suggest leads to potential sources of genealogical information.

A more detailed union catalogue of archival resources is provided by 'A2A' **www.a2a.org.uk**. Currently, 9,200,000 items from 408 English record offices are indexed. No doubt there will be more when you read this. Searching is by key word, and can be restricted to a particular record office or region, and also by date.

'Archives Hub' **www.archiveshub.ac.uk** is another union catalogue. It indexes archival collections held in higher education establishments. Universities and colleges often hold extensive archival collections, which may contain much of interest to genealogists. Some of this material may relate to their own areas, e.g. the archives of the Sneyds of Keele Hall at Keele University. Other collections, such as the Methodist Archives at the John Rylands Library in Manchester, are of national and even international importance. 'Archives Hub' provides links to the webpages of all the institutions whose archives it indexes. These pages often provide much more information than 'Archives Hub' itself.

Neither 'A2A' nor 'Archives Hub' index the two most important national collections of archives, namely the British Library and The National Archives. The only exception to this rule are the British Library's 'Asia Pacific and Africa Collections', listed by A2A **www.a2a.org.uk**, which include many personal collections related to British rule in India.

The British Library **www.bl.uk**, as well as being the second largest library in the world (and having one of the most extensive genealogical collections in the country) has an extensive collection of manuscripts. The full manuscripts catalogue is online (click 'manuscripts'). By clicking 'subject resources and links' you will also find pages on 'maps', 'newspapers', and the 'Oriental and India Office'. A wide range of other material is also available.

'The National Archives' website **www.nationalarchives.gov.uk** is one of the most useful sites available for U.K. genealogists, although (with the exception of its offshoot, the Family Records Centre) T.N.A. is not the record office of first resort for most family historians. Many T.N.A. pages have already been referred to. Beginners will want to start by clicking the 'I'm interested in . . . family history' button.

There are a number of buttons on the front page. Click 'research, education & online exhibitions' and 'Starting your Research'. This leads to 'getting started' guides on:

- Family history
- Local history
- House history
- Military history
- Palaeography
- Caring for your records

Another button on the 'research, education & online exhibitions' page leads to 'Research guides'. Here you will find links to numerous guides. These provide authoritative and often detailed discussions of particular topics covered by T.N.A's collections. Many have already been mentioned. There are far too many to list here, but leaflets of particular relevance are listed in the box.

National Archives Leaflets
- Bankruptcy and Insolvent Debtors 1710-1869
- Births, Marriages and Deaths at Sea
- Catholic Recusants
- Divorce Records after 1858 [also 'before']
- Domesday Book
- Enclosure Awards
- Hearth Tax 1662-1689
- Inquisitions Post Mortem, Henry III-Charles I: Landholders and their heirs
- Land Conveyances: Enrolment of Deeds, and Registration of Title
- Land Conveyances: Feet of Fines 1182-1833
- Manor and other Local Court Rolls, 13th century - 1922
- Medieval and Early Modern Sources for Family History
- Militia 1757-1914
- National Farm Surveys of England and Wales 1940-1943
- Old Bailey and the Central Criminal Court: Criminal Trials
- Passport Records
- Prisoners of War, British: 1939-1953
- Sources for Convicts and Prisoners 1100-1986
- Taxation Records before 1689
- Tracing 19th c. Criminals
- Tudor and Stuart Militia Muster Rolls
- Valuation Office Records: the Finance (1909-1910) Act

In addition, this button leads to 'In Depth Learning Guides' on 'Family history', 'Local history', 'Palaeography', and 'Beginners Latin'.

The 'Search the Archives' button leads to a number of pages, most of which have already been mentioned (A2A, Archon, census records, Documents Online, Hospital Records, Moving Here, and the National Register of Archives). The most impor-

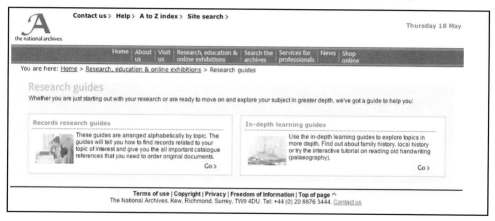

Plate 10. Guides on The National Archives website
www.nationalarchives.gov.uk provides much helpful information.
Crown copyright. Reproduced by permission of T.N.A. on behalf of the Controller of Her Majesty s Stationery Office.

tant page reached via this button, however, is the catalogue of T.N.A.'s archives. This includes 10,000,000 descriptions of documents from central government, courts of law, and other national organizations, including a huge amount of material likely to be of interest to the family historian. There is also a global search facility at **www.nationalarchives.gov.uk/search** which enables searches to be made across a range of T.N.A. databases.

The 'more' button gives access to

- the E179 database. This identifies 27,000+ lists of tax payers, dating from the twelfth to the seventeenth centuries.
- the 'Equity Pleadings Database'. This catalogues extensive records of civil cases in the seventeenth and eighteenth centuries, including many relating to wills, to property, and to debt.

- the 'Manorial Documents Register'. This is not confined to T.N.A. holdings, but gives the locations of manorial records in many other places. The online version is not yet complete.
- the list of 'Accessions to repositories'. New accessions to c.200 record offices are listed annually.
- the 'Trafalgar Ancestors' database, which provides details of all who fought at the Battle of Trafalgar in 1805.
- T.N.A's own reference library catalogue.

The web sites of county record offices cannot be expected to provide the same amount of information as T.N.A. Nevertheless, some of them are extensive. A number have their own catalogues online. Others refer you to A2A **www.a2a.org.uk**. Many have pages listing their holdings of parish registers, local newspapers, and census returns. Others have online databases of records in their possession. For example, 'Somerset Record Office' **www.somerset.gov.uk/archives** has databases of Somerset Estate Duty wills 1812-57, Bridgewater shipping crew lists, and prisoners in Ilchester Gaol, as well as a brief history of Somerset, and many guides to research. It has also digitised early Ordnance Survey maps of Somerset. 'Lincolnshire Archives' **www.lincolnshire.gov.uk/ archives** (click on 'Collections') has a number of online resources, including its 'Convicts Database', listing convicts transported to Australia, and 'Lindex: the Lincoln-shire Index', which indexes the contents of the *Stamford Mercury,* 1800-1899, as well as a wide range of other pub-lished sources. Gloucestershire's 'Genealogical Database' **www.gloucestershire.gov.uk/index.cfm?articleid=1335** indexes wills, 1541-1858, nonconformist baptisms, and gaol registers 1815-79. Cornwall Record Office **www.cornwall.gov.uk/cro** has a 'Gazetteer of Cornish Manors'. Its 'Cornwall Digital Tithe

Project' is digitising its tithe maps and apportionments (although none as yet are on its site). There is also a description of its 'Sources for the History of Medicine Project'.

Family History Societies
The last three decades have seen a rapid growth in the number of family history societies. The Federation of Family History Societies now has over 200 member societies. A full list of them is on its site at **www.ffhs.org.uk/General/ Members/index.htm**. 'Genuki' also has a links page at **www.genuki.org.uk/Societies**.

Family history societies undertake a wide variety of activities. These are usually described on their webpages. Most society pages include:

- details of membership
- information on the Society's journal (perhaps including contents lists)
- the society's programme of meetings and events
- research projects
- details of the society's library and resources
- a virtual bookshop for society publications
- links to other sites of interest
- the names of society officers

Sometimes there is more information than this. Many societies have notes on researching in their own areas. Some list the research interests of their members. A few offer lookups and search services. A small number offer online indexes, but many of these have been transferred to 'Family History Online' **www.familyhistoryonline.co.uk**.

The Society of Genealogists **www.sog.org.uk** is the largest genealogical society. It has one of the most significant genealogical libraries in the United Kingdom, only equalled in importance by the British Library. Its catalogue is of major significance, and is available online. A number of its major resources are now on the 'British Origins' site **www.britishorigins.com**. The Society's own website has a number of useful pages. Advice pages include:

- Genealogy as a Career
- The Right to Arms
- Has it been Done Before?
- Employing a Professional Researcher

The published listings of *County Sources in the Library of the Society of Genealogists* are also on the society's site.

The Federation of Family History Societies is the major umbrella organisation for family history societies. It aims to

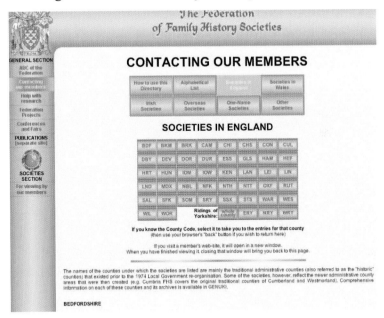

Plate 11. The Federation of Family History Societies directory www.ffhs.org.uk/General/Members will enable you to contact relevant family history societies.

co-ordinate the work of member societies, to organize collaborative projects, and to promote the interests of family historians generally. Some of the pages on its web site **www.ffhs.org.uk** have already been mentioned. A number of others deserve mention here. 'Research Services: a code of practice for beginners' **www.ffhs.org.uk/General/Help/Research.htm** describes the research services offered by family history societies, and explains how to make the best use of them. The 'National Strays Index' **www.ffhs.org.uk/General/Help/Strays.htm** is one of the Federation's major projects. It indexes names which are found in the records of places which are not the person's normal place of residence. 'Tracing the Birth Parents of Adopted Persons in England and Wales' **www.ffhs.org.uk/General/Help/Adopted.htm** is another useful page. The online book fair, 'Genfair' **www.genfair.com**, which is run by the Federation, will be discussed in chapter 8.

7. Solving Problem and Getting Help: Geography, Dates, Handwriting, Latin and Professionals

Where is that? When was that? Does that squiggle really mean something? What did this word mean? Who will help me solve these problems? These are questions which, sooner or later, all family historians using original sources will be faced with. Sources include the names of many obscure places. Dates are often given in ways which require translation into the modern calendar. Styles of handwriting have changed dramatically over the centuries. Anything written before the eighteenth century may not be easily readable. If it is in Latin, translation will also be required. Many of these problems can be solved with the help of webpages. If that proves not to be possible, or if you need research undertaken at a record office hundreds or thousands of miles away, you may need to employ a professional genealogist. The internet will enable you to find one.

Where was that? Gazetteers

Place-names found in original sources often provide useful clues for further genealogical research. If a source shows that an individual was living in a particular place, it is likely that other members of his or her family may be found within a few miles. The majority of placenames designate small places - villages, hamlets, even single houses. Many are likely to be unknown to you. Most, however, can be quickly identified by using gazetteers and maps. The latter may also show parish and other boundaries. These are important, since they may suggest where to look for records.

When consulting gazetteers, it is important to check their dates. The administrative areas mentioned in historic gazetteers have changed, sometimes dramatically, in the last century or so. The importance of these changes is discussed in the next section.

A variety of gazetteers are available on the internet. Not all of them can be mentioned here, but they are listed in *Family history on the web*. A number have links at Genuki's 'United Kingdom and Ireland Gazetteers' page **www.genuki.org.uk/ big/Gazetteers.html**. 'Genuki' itself has two separate gazetteers. The 'Genuki Gazetteer' **www.genuki.org.uk/big/ Gazetteer** covers the whole of the island of Great Britain and the Isle of Man. It includes the Ordnance Survey grid reference and the name of the parish, with a link to Genuki's parish page. The 'Genuki Church Database' **www.genuki.org.uk/big/ churchdb** lists churches located within a specified distance of a particular place. It also links to 'Genuki' parish pages.

'Genuki' also has a number of county gazetteers, e.g. for Devon **genuki.cs.ncl.ac.uk/DEV/Gazetteer** which tend to be much more detailed than the national gazetteers. In addition, it links to a large number of map sites, at all levels in its hierarchy. Some of its parish pages have their own maps. Devon and Sussex parish pages, for example, have detailed maps of parish boundaries drawn on old Ordnance Survey maps.

The Ordnance Survey's 'Place Name Gazetteer' is at **www.ordnancesurvey.co.uk/oswebsite/freefun/ didyouknow/index.html**. This indicates whether the place named is a village, town, forest, etc., gives its grid references and current local authority, and includes details of all current Ordnance Survey maps on which it is depicted. It also has some information on the meaning of place-names.

The best maps for family historians are probably from the Ordnance Survey 1:10,560 survey, published between 1844 and 1899. These are available at **www.old-maps.co.uk**. They show the landscape as it was before the twentieth century transformed it. The maps are consulted via a search mechanism. A search for 'South Street' revealed no less than 438 mentions! Consultation of this map should give you a better impression of how your ancestors may have viewed their surroundings. The map is also available at **www.british-history.ac.uk**, but there is no index on this site.

'Genmaps' **freepages.genealogy.rootsweb.com/~genmaps** is another useful map site. Its primary importance is that it has digitised thousands of historic maps, which are listed by county. These include maps ranging in coverage from whole counties to small villages. This site also has many links to other map sites. Many county maps may also be found at 'Your Maps Online' **www.yourmapsonline.org.uk**.

One site is devoted specifically to place names found in the census. 'Look for Places in the 1891 Census' **www.genuki.org.uk/big/census_place.html** can be used to identify the counties and registration districts in which places were situated. It also gives National Archives and Family History Library references for relevant census schedules.

London is a particularly difficult place to research. It has experienced numerous boundary changes. Many of its streets have experienced both changes of name and changes of direction. Harben's *Dictionary of London* **www.british-history.ac.uk/source.asp?pubid=3** tracks down many place names referred to in old documents. Gendoc's 'Victorian London A-Z Street Index' **homepage.ntlworld.com/hitch/gendocs/lon-str.html** locates 61,000 streets. Ivor Hoole has provided a 'Guide to the Courts Passages and Yards of Central London' **www.geocities.com/TheTropics/Cabana/9424**. Many old London maps have been digitised at the 'Collage' image database **collage.cityoflondon.gov.uk** (search for 'maps'). Hundreds of other London map sites may be found via search engines listed in chapter 3.

Where Was That: Administrative Areas

Family historians need an understanding of the administrative history of the areas their ancestors came from. The relationship of county, hundred, diocese, archdeaconry and parish is important, as it may determine where records may be found. A detailed discussion of 'British Counties, Parishes, etc., for Genealogists' is at **homepages.nildram.co.uk/~jimella/ counties.htm**. Reference may also be made to 'A Vision of Britain through Time' **www.visionofbritain.org.uk.**

The administrative history of the church is not as well served. However, some guidance can be found on Genuki's 'Cornwall: church history' page **www.genuki.org.uk/big/eng/ Cornwall/ChurchHistory.html**.

U.K. local government underwent many changes in the nineteenth and twentieth centuries. The 1974 changes were particularly important. Genuki's 'Local Government Changes in the United Kingdom' **www.genuki.org.uk/big/Regions/ UKchanges.html** describes some of the important features of these changes. It includes a table showing pre- and post-1974 counties, and their relationship with each other. A map of the historic 'Counties of England, Wales and Scotland prior to the 1974 Boundary Changes' is at **www.genuki.org.uk/big/Britain.html**.

Dates and Calendars

A wide range of methods of dating are used in original sources. Regnal years, saints days, Roman dating, and a variety of non-standard calendars were all frequently used. An overall view of various different calendars is found at the 'Frequently Asked Questions about Calendars' page **www.tondering.dk/**

claus/calendar.html. This includes an extended discussion of both Christian and Hebrew calendars, as well as much information on several others. A general guide to 'Chronology and dating' is at **www.medievalgenealogy.org.uk/guide/chron.shtml**.

Both of these sites mention the important change-over from the Julian to the Gregorian calendar in 1752, when Britain 'lost' eleven days. A more detailed discussion may be found at Mike Spathaky's page 'Old Style and New Style Dates and the Change to the Gregorian Calendar **www.genfair.com/dates.htm**. Julian calendar dates may be converted to Gregorian at the English Calendar' site **www.albion.edu/english/calendar/**.

This site has a number of other useful features. Calculators are provided for regnal years, for the dates of Easter and other major feast days, and for working out which days of the week particular dates fell upon.

Regnal years are commonly encountered in original sources. These are the years in which particular monarchs reigned. They are given in the form '1 George I'. This indicates the first year of the reign of George I, i.e. 1st August 1714-31st July 1715. A listing of 'English Regnal Years' is at **www.combs-families.org/combs/reference/regnal.htm**.

Another useful site is provided by Genuki's 'Dates of Easter Sunday and Perpetual Calendar, 1550-2049 for Great Britain and the Colonies' **www.genuki.org.uk/big/easter**. This site's prime function is to give full calendars for every year from 1550 to 2049, including the dates of Easter.

The use of saints days for dating was common in the medieval period. These are listed by the 'On-line Calendar of Saints Days' **medievalist.net/calendar/home.htm.**

More recently, Quakers refused to use the commonly accepted, but pagan, names of days and months. They adopted their own methods of dating. These are described in 'The Quaker calendar', which is one of the library guides issued by the 'Religious Society of Friends' **www.quaker.org.uk/ Templates/Internal.asp?NodeID=90037**.

Palaeography and Latin

The style of handwriting used in original sources prior to the mid-18th century is quite different to the style that is in use today. It may appear to be unreadable at first glance. But be comforted. It must have been written in order to be read! The ability to read old handwriting is a skill that needs practice. It must also be realised that our ancestors would have great problems reading modern handwriting.

The internet has two online tutorials on handwriting. The National Archives' 'Palaeography: reading old handwriting 1500-1800' **www.nationalarchives.gov.uk/palaeography/** is written with beginners in mind. Dave Postles page at **paleo.anglo-norman.org** is intended for students on the M.A. course in English local history at Leicester University. It includes separate sections on medieval and early-modern palaeography, and includes detailed bibliographies. It also includes documents in Latin.

Latin can be a serious obstacle to genealogical research. However, documents such as parish registers often follow a common form, and use the same words repeatedly. If you can work out the meanings of these words, then the battle may be won. An excellent online introduction is provided by The National Archives' 'Beginners Latin' tutorial **www.nationalarchives.gov.uk/latin/beginners**. Brief basic notes are provided by Genuki's 'Latin in Parish Records' **www.genuki.org.uk/big/LatinNotes.html**. The University of Notre Dame's 'Latin Dictionary and Grammar Aid' **www.nd.edu/~archives/latgramm.htm** may also be useful. It provides help with the grammatical endings of words which are often problematic for the beginner.

A number of glossaries and dictionaries are available. The Latin words likely to be found in genealogical sources are listed

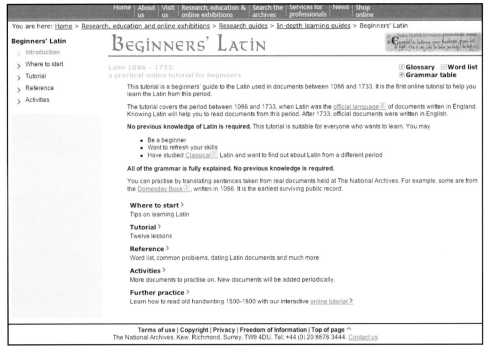

Plate 12. The National Archives Beginners Latin tutorial
www.nationalarchives.gov.uk/latin/beginners will help you to get started.
Crown copyright. Reproduced by permission of T.N.A. on behalf of the Controller of Her Majesty s Stationery Offce.

in the 'Latin Genealogical Word List' **www.familysearch.org/ Eng/Search/RG/guide/WLLatin.asp**. The authoritative published listing of medieval Latin words is C.T. Martin's *Record interpreter* (2nd ed. 1910). Its definitions include the Latin forms of many place and personal names. The book is reproduced on the 'White Trash Scriptorium' page **www.ipa.net/~magreyn**.

Professional Assistance

There are many ways of obtaining advice and help from others who share your interests. Some of them are discussed in chapter 9. There are also many professional genealogists offering to undertake research for a fee. If you reach a brick wall in your research, the records are 10,000 miles away, or you cannot cope with the Latin, then employing a professional is a reasonable option. Before you do, you should read the Society of Genealogists' page, 'Employing a professional researcher: a practical guide' **www.sog.org.uk/leaflets/researcher.pdf**.

It is most important to ensure that the person you employ has the expertise for the task in hand. It is therefore advisable to employ a member of the 'Association of Genealogists and Researchers in Archives' **www.agra.org.uk**. Its members are all well qualified researchers. They follow a professional code of practice.

Alternatively, the websites of record offices sometimes have lists of researchers with experience in their archives. The National Archives page on 'Independent Researchers' **www.nationalarchives.gov.uk/irlist**, for example, identifies experts in a wide range of documents. So does the National Archives of Ireland page on 'Genealogical & Historical Researchers' **www.nationalarchives.ie/genealogy/researchers.html**.

If you employ a researcher found on one of these lists, remember that he/she is a private individual. The record office cannot be held reponsible for the results obtained.

An increasing number of record offices are offering to undertake paid research for you. Details are given on their webpages.

8. Buying Books, CDs and Fiche Online

Books and other published materials are vital to genealogical research. Most, if not all, can be found in libraries (see chapter 6). However, it is worth building up a small bookshelf consisting of those works which you are likely to refer to constantly. At a minimum, this would include a good introductory guide to family history research, a genealogical dictionary, and historical bibliographies for the area(s) your ancestors lived in. You may also wish to purchase county-wide indexes of sources such as census schedules, marriage registers, trade directories, and similar materials, likely to contain data relevant to your ancestors.

Genealogical publishers may be divided into a number of categories:

- organizations which operate nationally, and publish a wide range of general guides to sources. This includes primarily the Federation of Family History Societies **www.ffhs.co.uk**, the Society of Genealogists **www.sog.org.uk/orderline** and The National Archives **www.nationalarchives.gov.uk/bookshop**. It also includes Phillimore **www.phillimore.co.uk**, the leading publisher of local history, whose titles frequently have genealogical relevance. Series such as the *National index of parish registers*, *British genealogical library guides* and the *Gibson guides* are indispensible, and have no effective equivalents on the internet.

- family history societies (see chapter 6). Their publications consist primarily of transcripts and indexes of original sources, especially census returns, parish registers and monumental inscriptions. These are mainly issued as booklets and microfiche, although the number of CDs issued by societies is increasing rapidly. Society webpages usually include a list of publications and an order form. In many cases, publications may also be ordered via 'Genfair' (see below).
- commercial CD publishers, who have re-issued innumerable out of print genealogical titles on CD. 'Archive CD Books' **www.archivecdbooks.org**, and 'S & N Genealogy Supplies' **www.genealogysupplies.com** are the leaders in this field. Many others regularly advertise in the genealogical press. Most nineteenth-century census schedules, and innumerable trade directories, are available on CD. So are many parish registers. The latter are rarely copied from the original registers. They are usually digitised images of published versions such as the *Phillimore parish registers* series.
- commercial microfiche publishers. 'Ancestral Indexes' **www.ancestral-indexes.co.uk,** and 'North Fiche' **www.jwillans.freeserve.co.uk** have both issued innumerable fiched transcripts and indexes of original sources for the northern counties.
- libraries and record offices. Many of these have published guides and handlists to their collections. Some have gone further, and published facsimiles and/or transcripts and indexes of original sources such as parish registers. Their publications are usually listed on their webpages (see chapter 6).

It is only possible to identify a few of the more important publishers here. There are numerous others, including both some main-stream commercial publishers, and many private individuals.

Some genealogical publications can be purchased in high street bookshops. For most, however, it is better to go to the specialists. Over 15,000 items can currently be purchased from the leading online genealogical fair, which brings together on the one site over 100 suppliers. 'Genfair' **www.genfair.com** is currently owned by the Federation of Family History Societies, although its future is uncertain. Its members make up the majority of 'stall-holders' although there are commercial 'stands' as well. The 'Parish Chest' **www.parishchest.com** is a similar virtual fair, with over 60 (mainly commercial) suppliers. A smaller range of books is carried by the National Archives' 'Bookshop' **www.nationalarchives.gov.uk/bookshop**.

If you are looking for a specific book, it is probably worth checking 'Amazon' **www.amazon.com**. 'Amazon' itself sells new books, but it also provides facilities for other booksellers to sell through its site. Hence it is possible to see prices for both new and second-hand books side by side. A similar service is provided by 'Alibris' **www.alibris.co.uk**.

There are also a number of sites which bring together the stock of a large number of different second-hand book sellers. These are listed in the box.

Second-Hand Books on the Web

• Abebooks **www.abebooks.co.uk**	• Fetch Book **www.fetchbook.info/**
• Addall **used.addall.com/**	• UK Book World **ukbookworld.com/**
• Biblioz.com **www.biblioz.com**	• Used Book Search **www.usedbooksearch.co.uk**

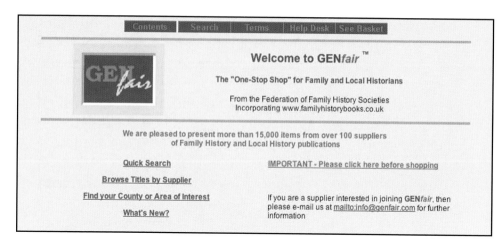

Contents | Search | Terms | Help Desk | See Basket

Welcome to GEN*fair* ™

The "One-Stop Shop" for Family and Local Historians

From the Federation of Family History Societies
Incorporating www.familyhistorybooks.co.uk

We are pleased to present more than 15,000 items from over 100 suppliers
of Family History and Local History publications

Quick Search

Browse Titles by Supplier

Find your County or Area of Interest

What's New?

IMPORTANT - Please click here before shopping

If you are a supplier interested in joining GEN*fair*, then please e-mail us at mailto:info@genfair.com for further information

Plate 13. Genfair **www.genfair.co.uk** offers a wide range of genealogical books and fiche from numerous different publishers

It is also worth checking 'eBay' **www.ebay.co.uk** occasionally. This is best known as an auction site, but there are a number of 'eBay' shops offering specialist genealogical services. Click on 'eBay stores' and type 'genealogy' into the search box for a list of stores. 'eBay' also auctions many genealogical books and CDs. To identify them, search for 'genealogy' in the main search box on eBay's front page. Make sure, however, that you are not infringing copyright by purchasing pirated CDs. Check that CD sellers have the right to sell the data they are supplying. It might also pay to search for the surnames you are researching, the places where your ancestors lived (especially counties), and the sources that you need to consult. If you have items you do not require, you can sell them on 'eBay' too.

There are also a number of genealogical booksellers who have their own sites. These are often on eBay as well. A few are listed below. Others can be identified in *Family history on the web.*

> **Genealogical Booksellers**
> - Family History Shop
>   **www.jenlibrary.u-net.com**
> - Internet Genealogical Bookshop
>   **www.stuartraymond.co.uk**
> - John Townsend Genealogy Books
>   **www.johntownsend.demon.co.uk**
>   Second-hand books
> - Ambra Books
>   **www.localhistory.co.uk/ambra**
>   Specialists in second-hand books from
>   South-West England

Many other second-hand booksellers, most of whom have some genealogical material, are listed on the 'Resources for Booksellers and Book Collectors' web-page at **www.2nd-hand-books.co.uk/sellers.html**.

Many printed books are available as digitised images online. The term 'e-book' has not been applied to many genealogical books online, but it is quite legitimate to regard, for example, the 'Historical Directories' site mentioned above (p. 61) as a collection of e-books. Nigel Batty-Smith's 'West Country genealogy' site **web.ukonline.co.uk/nigel.battysmith** has several 'e-books' taken from publications of the Harleian Society, reproducing pedigrees recorded by the heralds. Digitised images of the *Phillimore parish register series* have already been mentioned.

Most genealogical e-books are on the sites of private individuals. It is always worth typing the title of a book into a search engine such as **www.google.com**. Even if you do not find an e-book, you may locate a CD version, or even a bookseller who has the desired book in stock. Few genealogical books appear on the major e-book sites, such as 'Project Gutenburg' **www.gutenburg.org** or 'Google Book Search' **www.google.com/books.** But some can be found.

9. Obtaining More Help and Making Contact

Mailing Lists, Message Boards, & Newsgroups

Email is one of the most useful features of the internet. It enables you to make instant contact with others who share your interests. They may be able to offer you advice and assistance. They may even be tracing the same lines as you are.

Most websites include email addresses that may be useful. Family history societies, libraries and record offices may be prepared to provide email help and advice relating to their own interests and collections. Mailing lists are perhaps even more useful.

Mailing lists bring together people with a shared interest in a particular subject. An email sent to the list will reach every member of the group. A query posted on a mailing list is likely to be read by several hundred people, some of whom may have the answer. A brief introduction to the use of 'Genealogy Mailing Lists' can be consulted at **homepages.nildram.co.uk/ ~jimella/mail.htm**. Rootsweb provide a page on 'Mailing Lists: What are They?' at **helpdesk.rootsweb.com/help/ mail1.html**.

There are thousands of mailing lists relevant to British genealogists. They may be categorised by place, by surname, and by subject. Most are identified on Genuki's 'Genealogy Mailing Lists' page **www.genuki.org.uk/indexes/ MailingLists.html**. A comprehensive international listing is provided by Chris Gaunt and John Fuller's 'Genealogy Resources on the Internet' page **www.rootsweb.com/ ~jfuller/internet.html**.

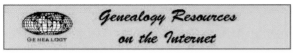

ENGLAND MAILING LISTS

URL: http://www.rootsweb.com/~jfuller/gen_mail_country-unk-eng.html

Last update: October 18, 2006 by John Fuller, johnf14246@aol.com

Register Resource | Update Resource | Report a Broken Link

- 74TH REGIMENT OF FOOT (74th Regiment of Foot, British regiment of the Revolutionary War)
- AngloIrish (Anglo-Irish ancestors in Ireland)
- ANGLO-ITALIAN (mixed English/Italian ancestry)
- BEDFORD (counties of Bedfordshire and Hertfordshire)
- BERKSHIRE (county of Berkshire)
- BIRKENHEAD (town of Birkenhead and the Wirral peninsula; formerly in Cheshire, now in Merseyside)
- BORDER (counties surrounding the border of Scotland and England)
- Bristol and Somerset (city of Bristol and county of Somerset)
- BUCKS (county of Buckinghamshire)
- CA-CORNISH (immigrants to California from Cornwall)
- CHESHIRE (county of Cheshire)
- CORNISH (general discussion of ancestors in Cornwall or emigrants from Cornwall)
- CORNISH-AMERICAN (emigrants from Cornwall, England, to the United States)
- CORNISH-ANCESTORS (announcement of updates to Cornish Ancestors Web Site)
- CORNISH-FAMILY (Cornwall)
- CORNISH-GEN (strict genealogy focus on ancestors in Cornwall or emigrants from Cornwall)
- CORNWALL-AUSTRALIA (immigrants from Cornwall to Australia)
- CORNWALL-TO-NZ (emigrants from Cornwall to New Zealand)
- cropredy (town of Cropredy, Oxfordshire)
- CUMBERLAND (county of Cumberland)
- dalesfhs (upper dales of Swaledale and Wensleydale, North Yorkshire)
- DERBYSGEN (county of Derbyshire)
- DEVON (county of Devon)
- DORSET (county of Dorset)
- downton (village of Downton, Wiltshire)
- DURHAM-1891 (volunteers transcribing 1891 census for Durham)
- DUR-NBL (County Durham and Northumberland)
- EAST-MARCHES (East Marches of England and Scotland)
- EastStonehouse-plymouth (parish of East Stonehouse, Devon)
- ENG-BANBURY-AREA (Banbury, Oxfordshire and adjacent areas)
- ENG-BFHS (Bedfordshire Family History Society)
- ENG-BKM-TINGEWICK (town of Tingewick, Buckinghamshire)
- ENG-BLACK-COUNTRY (Black Country towns of the English Midlands)
- ENG-BLACKCOUNTRY-DIASPORA (families who moved from Staffordshire/Worcestershire border to other counties)
- ENG-BRECKLAND (Breckland (Brecks) area of Suffolk and Norfolk)
- ENG-BUCKINGHAMSHIRE (county of Buckinghamshire)
- ENG-CAMBRIDGESHIRE (county of Cambridgeshire)
- ENG-CAM-LINTON (Linton registration district, Cambridgeshire)
- ENG-CANAL-PEOPLE (boat people of England's inland waterways)
- ENG-CHS-KNUTSFORD (town of Knutsford, Cheshire, and surrounding districts)

Plate 14. Innumerable mailing lists are held on the Genealogy resources on the Internet page
www.rootsweb.com/~jfuller/gen_mail_country-unk-eng.html.

Almost 30,000 mailing lists may be found on Rootsweb's 'Mailing list' page **lists.rootsweb.com**. Although the majority are North American, a substantial minority are of interest to British researchers. This includes numerous lists for British places - not just regions and counties, but also towns and villages. It also includes thousands of surname lists, and lists on specific topics such as the Boer War, railwaymen, and the census. A variety of lists can also be found at 'Yahoo Groups' **groups.yahoo.com**.

In order to join a mailing list, you have to subscribe. This sometimes involves filling in an online form. Alternatively, you may have to send an email to the computer that manages the list. Details of how to do this are usually given on mailing list webpages. The email that you send to subscribe to a list should not be used to send messages to the list: it will not get through. An introductory email can be sent when you receive the usual welcome message, which will have details of how to contact the group. Subscription to a mailing list does not involve payment.

Some mailing lists have restricted membership. This applies particularly to those run by family history societies, who may restrict the list to their own members. If there is a moderator, he/she may be able to control who joins. Other lists may be restricted to those working on a particular project. A few lists are restricted to announcements. For example, the Society of Genealogists' 'Sog-News-L' **www.sog.org.uk/online/lists.html#news** is for announcements about the society and its activities, not for discusssion.

Messages from mailing lists can be received in two ways. You can ask for them to be sent 'mail mode', in which case you will receive each message as a separate email. Alternatively, they can be grouped together in a 'digest'. Digests include a number of messages in one email, and may help to prevent your email box becoming clogged up.

Message boards provide a similar service, but do not use email: messages are posted on-site only. The distinction between the two is, however, decreasing. Mailing lists usually display their messages on web sites as well as posting e-mails, and some sites which were formerly pure message boards now send e-mails as well.

Message boards for every county in the British Isles are available on the 'Ancestry' site **boards.ancestry.com**. Many of these link to Rootsweb mailing lists. The 'B-G Forums' page **www.british-genealogy.com/forums** hosts many lists of UK interest, on a variety of topics. It includes forums for every county in England, Scotland and Wales. 'Rootschat' **www.rootschat.com** has a similar range of forums. 'Genforum' has many surname lists at **genforum.genealogy.com/index.html**. 'Curious Fox' **www.curiousfox.com** is a particularly useful message board. It has pages for every county, town, and village in the U.K., where queries can be placed.

Newsgroups are another internet sub-species. They are similar to message boards, but require special software to read. This is provided with browsers such as Internet Explorer or Netscape Navigator. Nowadays, most of their messages can also be found on mailing lists. Their advantage is that you do not need to subscribe to the list (and hence receive many emails), but can simply call the messages up whenever you wish. Usenet newsgroups are listed on the 'Genealogy Resources on the Internet' page **www.rootsweb.com/~jfuller/internet.html**.

Mailing lists and newsgroups generally maintain archives of past messages. These may be searched for specific information, or browsed to get a flavour of what the list is about before subscribing. Rootsweb list archives can be searched at **archiver.rootsweb.com**. The archives of Usenet newsgroups can be searched from **groups.google.com**. The main 'Google' search engine **www.google.com** automatically searches Usenet.

Which lists should you use? There are many to choose from. There are several dozen lists devoted to the entire field of English genealogy. Numerous lists are devoted to particular counties, and also to towns and villages within them. There are likely to be surname lists for some at least of the names you are researching. It may not be easy to decide which is the best for you.

What do you want to use a list for? Do you just want to 'lurk', to read messages without taking part? Do you want to ask questions? Do you have the knowledge to answer questions? The nature of your interests will help to determine how you use these lists.

Start by reading list archives. That will give you the 'flavour' of a list. It will enable you to see the nature of topics that are discussed. Reading the list archives of a surname list, for example, will show you whether it is dominated by American interests - as many are. Notice how many members a list has, and how many messages are sent to the list each month. Ask yourself how many you could cope with.

Lists devoted to the surnames you are researching are the obvious lists to join. So are the lists for the counties, towns and villages in which your ancestors lived. If you have specific questions about a particular source, or an occupation, then you may want to use lists devoted to those topics. The many general lists offer an opportunity to pick up tips at a wider level. Bear in mind that it is easy to subscribe and unsubscribe to mailing lists. You can do so as frequently as you wish.

The best results from using mailing lists will be obtained by using relevant lists. Be careful that you ask questions about Cornwall on lists that deal with Cornwall, rather than Northumberland. There is no point asking a question about a particular surname on a list dealing with computer issues. Off-topic questions should be avoided, as they can be annoying to other members.

The most important part of your message is the subject heading. This needs to be as specific as possible. Messages that just say 'family history' are unlikely to be read. An enquiry headed 'Cuttlesham', however, will be read by everyone who is likely to know anything about the place. That may not be very many people, but will include any members who have detailed knowledge. Surnames are likely to attract attention from anyone researching the same name. If the list is devoted to a particular surname, you will need to be more specific.

Do not ask questions that are answered in a mailing list's own 'F.A.Q.' (frequently asked questions) page. There are certain questions which are likely to be repeated ad nauseum on any list, to the annoyance of regular list members. The F.A.Q. page is designed to answer them so that there is no need for them to be asked on the list. You should read it.

Similarly, don't ask questions that could be easily answered from a good genealogy textbook, or by searching the web. For example, many messages ask where a particular place is. The gazetteers mentioned in chapter 7 will usually answer such questions. Similarly, the opening times of a particular record office will usually be shown on its webpage, and does not require a mailing list inquiry. Don't let your laziness show on mailing lists!

It is important to avoid rudeness. Never send an instant angry response to a message. If you do, you will regret it. Bear in mind, too, that messages will be read by the whole membership. If your message just concerns a particular member, send it to him or her - nobody else wants to read it. And when you 'reply' to messages, remember to delete the message you are replying to in the text of your email. Failure to do this makes mailing list digests much harder to read.

The advice offered above summarises commonly accepted guidelines for users of mailing lists and newsgroups, which is often referred to as 'netiquette'. A more detailed discussion of netiquette may be found at the 'Netiquette Home Page' **www.albion.com/netiquette**. The 'Notes on List Etiquette' at **www.mno.org.uk/letiquette** may also be useful.

Surname Sites

Mailing lists for specific surnames provide one means of contacting others who are researching your surnames. There are a variety of other means available on the internet. Interest lists, pedigree databases and personal web sites all provide information for researchers investigating particular surnames. You should check each of these three categories, and consider participating in them personally. Advertising your own interests on the internet is likely to enable you to make more contacts than you otherwise could.

Interest Lists

Numerous lists of surname interests are available, both on the web, and in printed format. Most family history societies regularly publish lists in their journals. Some have created web-pages for them. Many county-wide interest lists are hosted by 'Genuki'. These and others are listed on Genuki's 'Surname lists' page **www.genuki.org.uk/indexes/SurnamesLists.html**. This links to the important 'Online English Names Directory' **www.list.jaunay.com/engnames**. Another useful site is 'UK Surnames' **www.county-surnames.co.uk**, which has pages for every county in the United Kingdom. These pages can usually be found from Genuki's county pages.

The largest interests list on the internet is 'Rootsweb Surname List' **rsl.rootsweb.com**. This is heavily biased towards North American researchers. Nevertheless, it is international in scope.

The 'Register of One Name Studies' **www.one-name.org/ register.shtml** is also important. This lists 7,000 surnames registered with the Guild of One Name Studies. The researchers who have registered them are all committed to collecting all occurrences of the surname on a world-wide basis. They are therefore likely to be the leading experts on the particular name. If one of these names is yours, you should make contact.

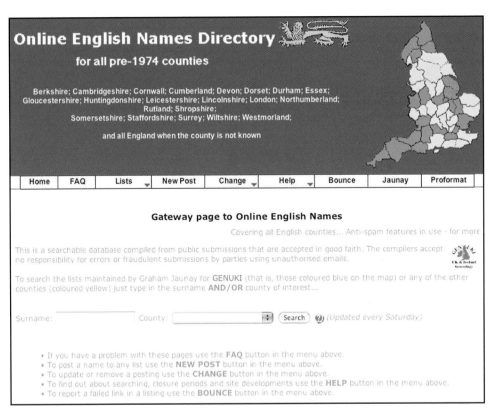

Plate 15. Surname interest lists enable you to make contact with other researchers. There are lists for many counties on the Online English Names directory **www.list.jaunay.com/engnames.**

Pedigrees

The internet has a number of pedigree databases which enable you to add your own details. You do not need to have your own webpage to place your pedigree online. Most of these databases accept GEDCOM data, which is produced by most pedigree database programmes. GEDCOM is the accepted standard file format for computerised pedigrees.

The majority of pedigree databases on the internet are biased towards research in North America. Nevertheless, they are international in scope, and contain a huge amount of British data.

One of the most useful of these databases is Ancestry's 'World Tree' **www.ancestry.com/trees/awt/main.aspx**. Although it is commercially sponsored, there is no cost for a search. Its pages provide basic genealogical data on each individual recorded. Its advantage over other databases is that much detailed personal information can be given. It also leads to a page which gives a distribution map for every surname recorded in the 1891 census.

'Family search' **www.familysearch.org** has two major pedigree databases. 'Ancestral file' has a separate record for each individual named, giving basic genealogical information, plus a pedigree chart showing family relationships. The 'Pedigree Resource File' has an 'individual record' giving details of birth, parentage, and/or marriage.

Rootsweb's 'World Connect' **worldconnect.rootsweb.com** is another substantial database, with over 350 million names. 'Gencircles' **www.gencircles.com** is much smaller. It enables others to add information to the pedigree that you have posted.

'Lost cousins: putting relatives in touch' **www.lostcousins.com** is a different type of database. It does not require you to enter the whole of your pedigree. Rather, you are asked to identify your ancestors in the 1881 census. If any other researcher identifies the same ancestors, you will be put in touch.

None of these databases charges a fee at the moment. There are, however, a number of subscription databases worth joining. 'Genserv' **www.genserv.com** requires participants to both upload their own pedigree data, and to pay a subscription. 'World Family Tree' **familytreemaker.genealogy.com/wfttop.html** permits you to undertake searches for free, but will not reveal the full results until you have paid a subscription. It has over 180 million names. 'Genes Re-united' **www.genesreunited.com** is smaller - over 34 million names - but similar, except that it has a UK bias. It lists names, birthplaces, and dates of birth and death. A subscription has to be paid if you wish to obtain further details from the submitter.

'One Great Family' **www.onegreatfamily.com** has 190 million names. Its pedigrees are submitted by clients, but are automatically merged when the computer detects a connection.

All of these databases rely on the information supplied by submitters. There is no check on that information. Frequently, information on the same individual has been submitted several times. In some cases, variations in the information given by different submitters show that a thorough check against the original sources is needed. Nevertheless, the information provided may enable you to establish whether individuals named are in your own line of descent. If so, then it is likely to be worth contacting submitters.

Personal Websites: Your Own

Innumerable family historians have published their own websites. This is something that you may want to consider doing when you have useful information to publicise. A website is likely to attract contact from others researching the same family. Your own website has a number of advantages over using a pedigree database:

- you can use it to record your family history, not just your genealogy. Most pedigree databases only give you room for a pedigree, not for other biographical information.
- it will be found by a search engine. The information in pedigree databases will not.
- you have control over the content of your own web page. That is not necessarily the case with a pedigree database.

Creating your own webpage is not difficult. A basic introduction is given in chapter 17 of Peter Christian's book, *The genealogists internet* (3rd ed. National Archives, 2005). Kylie Macrae's *Haynes internet genealogical manual* (Hayne Publishing, 2005) is primarily an instruction manual for genealogical webpage designers. 'Cyndi's Genealogy Home Page Construction Kit' **www.cyndislist.com/construc.htm** provides useful guidance on the task of designing a webpage. The text of Peter Christian's *Web publishing for genealogy* (2nd ed. David Hawgood, 1999) is also available online **www.spub.co.uk/wpg/index.html**, although now rather dated.

Personal Websites: How to Find Them

A search for your family name on a search engine may well reveal a number of webpages relating to your surname. It is also likely to bring up many irrelevant sites. There are a number of index pages which are worth checking before using search engines. The 'Registry of Websites at Rootsweb' **www.rootsweb.com/~websites** lists many thousand surname pages. Cyndi's 'Personal Home Pages Index' **www.cyndislist.com/personal.htm** also links to thousands of sites. Both of these indexes are biased towards North American research. For specifically English sites, the 'A-Z of Family Surnames from England' **members.tripod.com/~Caryl_Williams/names-7.html** should be consulted.

Finding People

It may be that you have lost contact with relatives or with others whom you think could provide information on your family history. There are a variety of ways to find them on the internet.

Email is an obvious way to contact people. Unfortunately, finding email addresses is not easy. There is no single directory of all email addresses. It is possible to use a search engine to search for a person's name, which may reveal an email address as well. There are a substantial number of email directories for specific purposes. These are listed at **uk.dir.yahoo.com/ Reference/Phone_Numbers_and_Addresses/Email_Addresses**. Such directories may not give accurate information, since email addresses tend to change frequently. Email address databases are unlikely to be informed of changes, so they are often full of out of date information.

Many sites listing phone numbers are available. These are usually commercial sites, but offer a small number of free searches. They can be found by using search engines. Amongst the most popular are:

- The Phone Book
  www.thephonebook.bt.com/
- 192.com
  www.192.com
- 118118.com
  www.118118.com

Tracing people through the phone directory is bedevilled by the fact that an increasing proportion of phone subscribers are ex-directory. An alternative is provided by electoral registers. Again, a number of sites offer searches, usually fee-based:

- 192.com
  www.192.com/search
- Locate First.com
  www.locatefirst.com
- LookupUK.com
  www.lookupuk.com
- Tracesmart
  www.tracesmart.co.uk
- UK Name and Address Tracer
  www.nametracer.co.uk

Some of these also offer a variety of tracing services. An overview of resources and services for 'Tracing Living People' is provided by the British Library **www.bl.uk/collections/social/spis_tlp.html**. Cyndi's 'Finding people' page **www.cyndislist.com/finding.htm** links to a variety of other potentially useful pages.

10. Ireland

Ireland became a Kingdom in 1541. It has always had its own government(s), despite the fact that it was a part of the United Kingdom between 1801 and 1922, during which time it had no parliament of its own. In 1922, the southern counties became a dominion within the British Empire. Subsequently (in 1948) they became the Republic of Ireland. Northern Ireland remained within the United Kingdom, and had its own Parliament for most of the twentieth century.

Irish governments created their own records. Those which survive are mostly in the National Archives of Ireland **www.nationalarchives.ie** or the Public Record Office of Northern Ireland **www.proni.gov.uk**. Neither institution provides an online catalogue of its holdings. Their sites do, however, provide a great deal of useful information for the family historian. For example, the Public Record Office site has extensive 'Introductions to the Major (Private) Archives' **www.proni.gov.uk/records/USING/using.htm**. Its 'Prominent Persons Index' **www.proni.gov.uk/records/ private/ppi.htm** provides information on 5,000 people who are represented in the Office's collections. Several other pages from these two sites will be mentioned below.

Researchers in Ireland are faced with more difficulties than those in the rest of the British Isles. Numerous records were lost in 1922, when the Irish Public Record Office was destroyed. The destruction included many Church of Ireland parish registers, most nineteenth century census schedules, and a large number of wills.

Everything, however, was not lost. Many other records do survive. A variety of introductory guides are available on the internet. The 'Fianna guide to Irish genealogy' **www.rootsweb.com/~fianna** offers over 500 pages of information and advice. It has a small number of transcriptions from primary sources. 'Moving Here', the site for immigrants to England, has a section devoted to 'Irish Roots' **www.movinghere.org.uk/galleries/roots/irish/irish.htm**, written by John Grenham. The 'Irish Ancestors' site **www.ireland.com/ancestor** has many pages introducing specific sources, and listing resources for particular counties. Genuki's 'Ireland' section **www.genuki.org.uk/big/irl** provides much helpful advice, many links, and county pages listing resources. Other 'county' pages can be found on the 'Ireland Genweb Project' **www.irelandgenweb.com** as well as on the 'Fianna' and 'Irish Ancestors' sites mentioned above.

These county pages offer much useful advice. They link to a wide range of transcripts and indexes of primary sources. Information is provided on local libraries, record offices, and family history societies.

Ireland is also provided with a network of genealogical research centres able to carry out research in some of the major sources - which are not always available for personal research. The 'Irish Family History Foundation' **www.irish-roots.net** provides a gateway to the websites of these centres.

The first source genealogists need to consult are the civil registers. In Ireland, civil registration began in 1845, although until the end of 1863 only non-Roman Catholic marriages were recorded. A number of webpages describe the records. The best is probably the 'State Registration of Births, Marriages and Deaths' section of the 'Irish Ancestors' site **scripts.ireland.com/ancestor/browse/records/state**. Reference might also be made to 'A Guide to the

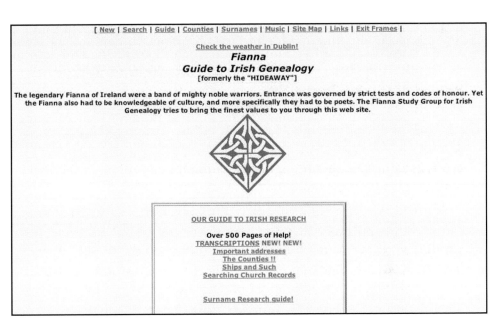

[New | Search | Guide | Counties | Surnames | Music | Site Map | Links | Exit Frames |

Check the weather in Dublin!

Fianna
Guide to Irish Genealogy
[formerly the "HIDEAWAY"]

The legendary Fianna of Ireland were a band of mighty noble warriors. Entrance was governed by strict tests and codes of honour. Yet the Fianna also had to be knowledgeable of culture, and more specifically they had to be poets. The Fianna Study Group for Irish Genealogy tries to bring the finest values to you through this web site.

OUR GUIDE TO IRISH RESEARCH

Over 500 Pages of Help!
TRANSCRIPTIONS NEW! NEW!
Important addresses
The Counties !!
Ships and Such
Searching Church Records

Surname Research guide!

Plate 16. The Fianna guide to Irish genealogy www.rootsweb.com/~fianna provides much helpful information to the Irish researcher.

General Register Office of Ireland' **homepage.eircom.net/ ~seanjmurphy/gro**, which includes a list of registration districts. The registers themselves are in the custody of the Irish General Register Office **www.groireland.ie**.

From 1922, the responsibility for civil registers in Northern Ireland was accepted by the 'General Register Office (Northern Ireland)' **www.groni.gov.uk**. This office also holds some (but not all) pre-1922 registers. Full details are given on their web site.

There is no online access to the registers in either of these offices. It is likely to be some years before indexes become available on the internet. Some indexes, however, have been microfilmed for the Latter-Day Saints. Details are given on Family Search's 'Ireland Research Outline' page **www.familysearch.org** (click on 'search', 'research helps', and use the alphabetical list). A variety of indexes for many registration districts may be found at From Ireland's 'Civil Records: Birth, Marriage & Death Registration' page **www.from-ireland.net/gene/ civilregistration.htm** (click on 'civil registration districts). The registers held by district registrars have not so far been indexed on the web. The only exception to this rule is Waterford County Library's 'Death Registers' **www.waterfordcountylibrary.ie/library/web?task=Display&art_id=2**, covering 1864-1901.

Prior to the introduction of civil registration, baptisms, marriages and burials were recorded in parish registers. The Church of Ireland was the established church until 1922, but it had far fewer adherents than the Roman Catholic church. Presbyterians were strong in Northern Ireland. There were also a few other denominations: Baptist, Methodist, Quaker, and others. All of these kept registers of baptisms, marriages and burials. Fianna's 'Churches and Searches' page **www.rootsweb.com/~fianna/county/churches.html** provides information about the registers of a variety of denominations active in Ireland.

Unfortunately, the majority of Church of Ireland (i.e., Anglican) registers were destroyed in 1922. Information about surviving registers is given on the 'Church of Ireland Genealogy and Family History' page **www.ireland.anglican.org/ library/libroots.html**. There is a guide to 'Useful Genealogical Sources: Parochial Records and Marriage Licences' **www.nationalarchives.ie/genealogy/church.html** on the 'National Archives of Ireland' site. This site also has a list of 'Church of Ireland Parish Registers: Surrogates', i.e.transcripts and abstracts of registers, available in the National Archives **www.nationalarchives.ie/PDF/CofIReplacements.pdf**.

Many parish registers are still held by clergy. Some are also held by the Representative Church Body Library, by the National Archives of Ireland, and by the Public Record Office of Northern

Ireland. A listing of the latter's microfilm is provided on its 'Church of Ireland Index' at **www.proni.gov.uk/records/ private/cofiindx.htm**. It is intended to film all registers, but this has not yet been done.

Roman Catholic registers do survive. Many are held on microfilm by both the National Archives of Ireland and the Public Record Office of Northern Ireland. Lists are given on both their webpages. A comprehensive list of registers and their locations is given on Irish Ancestors' 'Roman Catholic records' page **scripts.ireland.com/ancestor/browse/counties/rcmaps**.

Many Presbyterian registers have been microfilmed by the Public Record Office of Northern Ireland. These are listed on its 'Index to Presbyterian Church Records' page **www.proni.gov.uk/records/private/presindx.htm**. The Latter-Day Saints Family History Library also has microfilms of many Irish parish registers of all denominations. For these, consult Fianna's 'L.D.S. Film Numbers for Ireland Parish Registers' page **www.rootsweb.com/~fianna/county/ ldspars.html**.

Apart from the I.G.I., there are no major databases containing indexes or transcripts of information from parish registers. However, quite a number of pages deal with particular parishes. These can often be found through the 'county' pages mentioned above. Rootsweb's 'User Contributed Databases' **userdb.rootsweb.com/regional.html** also has a number of parish indexes (click on 'Irl', and on 'United Kingdom'). A comprehensive listing is given in Raymond's *Irish family history on the web.*

'County' pages also list many transcripts and indexes of monumental inscriptions from particular cemeteries and graveyards. One of the larger Irish databases is devoted to 'Ireland's Gravestone Index' **www.irishgenealogy.ie/ gravestones**, which indexes almost 400,000 inscriptions from over 850 cemeteries. 'Interment.net' **www.interment.net**

which has already been mentioned in the English context, also has an important Irish collection. Tombstone inscriptions recorded in the nineteenth century may be searched, for a fee, at 'Irish Memorials of the Dead' **www.ajmorris.com/dig/toc/memdead.htm**.

It has already been noted that most nineteenth-century census records have been lost. However, the records for 1901 and 1911 do survive. The originals are held by the National Archives of Ireland, and are open for inspection. Microfilm is available at the Public Record Office of Northern Ireland, at the Latter Day Saints Family History Library, and at various other institutions. The webpages of these institutions (see above) provide details of what is available. It is also worth reading Fianna's 'Censuses' page **www.rootsweb.com/~fianna/guide/census.html**. This includes a page on 'Census substitutes'.

Digitisation of these census records is under way, although images are not available online at the time of writing. A number of small census databases are currently available. The most substantial of these are the 'Leitrim Roscommon 1901 Census Home Page' **www.leitrim-roscommon.com/1901census**, and the '1901 Census of Population of Co Clare' **www.clarelibrary.ie/eolas/coclare/genealogy/1901census/1901_clare_census.htm.** There are also a few transcripts and/or indexes for smaller areas, many of them listed at 'Irish Census Records' **www.censusfinder.com/irish-census-records5.htm**.This page also lists a number of pages offering transcripts and/or indexes of various substitutes for the lost censuses.

Two major sources can be used as census substitutes. The tithe applotment books, compiled between 1823 and 1837, record the names of all occupiers who were liable to pay tithes. These books are effectively lists of heads of households. The originals are in the National Archives of Ireland and the Public

Record Office of Northern Ireland (both of whose websites offer helpful introductions). Many books for particular parishes are available on the internet.

Secondly, Griffith's Valuation provides a survey of property for all Irish counties. It was made between 1848 and 1864, and lists every land owner and occupier. Its purpose was to serve as a basis for tax assessments. A full database, with scanned images of the original returns, is available at 'Irish Origins'. See its 'Griffiths Valuation 1847-1864' page **www.irishorigins.com/ help/popup-aboutio-grif.htm**. There are also many indexes and/or transcripts for particular parishes and counties. For example, nineteen Donegal parishes are included on the '1857 Griffiths Valuation of Co. Donegal' page **freepages.genealogy.rootsweb.com/~donegal/griffiths.htm**.

Earlier 'census substitutes' include the registers of freeholders entitled to vote in elections, and the poll books which record who voted in Parliamentary elections. The Public Record Office of Northern Ireland has digitised and indexed more than 5,500 pages from freehold registers and poll books of the eighteenth and early nineteenth centuries on its 'Freeholders Records' page **www.proni.gov.uk/freeholders**.

The 'Ulster Covenant' **www.proni.gov.uk/ulstercovenant** is another major database on the Public Record Office of Northern Ireland site. Just under half a million people signed this declaration against Home Rule in 1912. This index enables their signatures to be identified, and their addresses to be located. This provides a useful check on the 1911 census for Northern Ireland.

For English and Scottish researchers, probate records provide invaluable information. Unfortunately, many Irish wills were lost in 1922. Some, however, remain. There are also some indexes and abstracts of the lost wills. The Irish Ancestors' 'Wills' page **scripts.ireland.com/ancestor/browse/records/ wills** provides a detailed introduction to researching Irish wills. Sherry Irvine's two articles on 'Probate in Ireland' **www.ancestry.com/learn/library/article.aspx?article=2515** are also useful. Irish Origins 'Irish wills index' **www.irishorigins.com/ help/popup-aboutio-wills.htm** indexes many of the destroyed wills. Indexes are also available at 'Digdat: Digital Irish Data' **www.ajmorris.com/dig/toc/titlres.htm**.

The destruction of the Irish Public Record Office was a minor episode in the history of the sufferings of Ireland. The Great Famine of 1845-50 was of much greater significance. 'Sources in the National Archives for researching the Great Famine' **www.nationalarchives.ie/topics/famine/famine.html** describes the records available in the National Archives of Ireland for researching this disaster.

The famine forced millions to flee their homes. But it was not the only reason for Irish emigration. Many of the websites mentioned above include information on Irish emigrants throughout the nineteenth century. Another useful source is the 'Ireland-Australia transportation database' **www.nationalarchives.ie/topics/transportation/search01.html**.

A wide range of other Irish databases are available on the internet. A number of sites offer substantial collections of mainly small databases. These include:

> • Ancestry.com's 'Ireland' section
> **www.ancestry.com/search/locality/ dbpage.aspx?tp=3257&p=3250**.

Ancestry.com has already been mentioned. It has a small number of Irish databases. One of these is the 'Irish Flax Growers List 1796', which lists no less than 56,000 flax growers. Another is its 'Irish wills index', noted above.

- DIGdat: Digital Irish Genealogical Data
  www.ajmorris.com/dig/index.htm

DIGdat's wills indexes have already been mentioned. It also has a number of local indexes to Griffith's Valuation, some pedigree databases, and a variety of other material covering small areas.

- Irish Family Research
  www.irishfamilyresearch.co.uk.

Most of the indexes on this site cover small areas. They include Griffith's Valuation, trade directories, flax growers lists, school registers, Yeomanry lists, births, marriage and death announcements in newspapers, and a variety of other sources.

- Irish Origins
  www.irishorigins.com

The Irish section of 'British Origins' , It has a complete index to the important Griffith's Valuation of 1847-64, an 'Index of Irish wills, 1484-1858' at the National Archives of Ireland, an index of passenger lists for 1890, and a variety of census and other databases.

- A Little Bit of Ireland
  www.celticcousins.net/ireland/.

Indexes on this site mostly relate to Clare, Galway, Limerick, Mayo, and Roscommon. There are also indexes to marriages in *Walkers Hibernian magazine,* 1771-1812, and to a number of other newspapers.

A wide range of other pages are available. Many of them relate to particular parishes or other small areas, and record a number of sources. These can be found through the 'county pages' mentioned above. Over 1,500 webpages are listed in *Irish family history on the web,* which should be used as a companion volume to this chapter.

Further Reading

DAVIS, BILL. *Irish ancestry: a beginners' guide.* 3rd ed. F.F.H.S., 2001.

GRENHAM, JOHN. *Tracing your Irish ancestors.* 3rd ed. Dublin: Gill & Macmillan, 2006.

RAYMOND, STUART A. *Irish family history on the web.* 3rd ed. Family History Partnership, forthcoming.

11. Scotland

The Kingdom of Scotland did not become a part of the United Kingdom until 1707, although the crowns were united in 1603. It has its own system of government. Genealogical records in Scotland differ from those in England in many respects.

The most substantial internet guide to Scottish genealogy is provided by 'Mother Hubbard's Cupboard' **www.niteo.org/vhs/diana/genclass/205/gen205.htm**. There are also many helpful pages at 'Family Search' **www.familysearch.org** (click on 'search', 'research helps', and 'S'). Most net-based introductory guides are fairly brief. The B.B.C.'s 'Scottish roots' site **www.bbc.co.uk/scotland/history/scottishroots** has pages on 'Getting started' 'further steps', 'initial sources' and 'digging deeper'. 'Genuki' has extensive information, but only offers a brief 'Introduction to Scottish Family History' **www.genuki.org.uk/big/sct/intro.html**.

Scotland has a range of record offices and local studies libraries. 'Scottish Record Offices and Archives on the Web' **www.oz.net/~markhow/scotsros.htm** provides a gateway to their web sites, designed for family historians. The 'Scottish Archive Network' **www.scan.org.uk** provides a more comprehensive directory. It also also includes an online catalogue, which is the Scottish equivalent of 'A2A' . This catalogue lists the holdings of 52 Scottish record offices. If you want to go beyond the information provided by 'Scotland's People' (see below), you will need to consult this catalogue.

The 'National Archives of Scotland' **www.nas.gov.uk** holds the records of Scottish central government. It has an online catalogue of its holdings, although this is not yet complete. It also has a page on 'Family History', describing what it holds and what it does not hold. It should be noted that some of the most important records for genealogists - civil registers, the census, the old parish registers - are held by the General Register Office for Scotland (see below), not by The National Archives of Scotland. The two institutions are due to merge in the near future.

The National Archives of Scotland also runs the 'National Register of Archives for Scotland' **www.nas.gov.uk/nras**. Its 'register' lists the holdings of private archives.

Most researchers are likely to begin their research with the 'Scotlands People' website **www.scotlandspeople.gov.uk** This single site offers databases of the four most important sources for Scottish genealogy. If all you want to do is to construct your pedigree, then you may need to look no further! This site has the civil (statutory) registers, the old parish registers, the census 1871-1901, and Scottish wills. It is a pay per view site. Once you have paid to see a particular document, you can view it online as frequently as you like without paying any more.

Scottish civil registration began in 1855. 'Scotlands People' includes the indexes to births 1855-1904, marriages 1855-1929, and deaths 1855-1914, together with digitised images of the original registers. Later registers are not included due to privacy concerns, but each year one more year's register will be added.

Certificates for the periods not covered by 'Scotlands People' can be purchased from the 'General Register Office for Scotland' **www.gro-scotland.gov.uk**. However, they cannot be ordered online. Click on 'Family Records' for details of ordering procedures. This site includes much useful information on the Office's other records, which include census schedules and old parish registers. It also has a list of 'parishes and registration districts' **www.gro-scotland.gov.uk/famrec/ hlpsrch/list-of-parishes-registration-districts.html**, which will be useful if you wish to search the registers of district registrars.

'Scots Origins' **www.scotsorigins.com** provide an alternative means of obtaining civil registration information. Transcripts of the civil registers may be ordered as 'Origins expert transcriptions' via the internet. These are also available for information from the old parish registers, and from the 1861 and 1871 censuses.

The Scottish civil registers contain more information than their English equivalent. For example, in 1855, and from 1861 onwards, Scottish birth registers record the ages and birthplaces of a child's parents. Marriage certificates record the maiden names of each spouse's mother.

Scotland's old parish registers have been collected together and housed centrally. This has made it much easier to index and digitise them. Full indexes are available at 'Scotlands People'. Digitised images are likely to be available soon.

The old parish registers do not provide a complete record of Scottish baptisms marriages and burials. There were a variety of denominations active in Scotland other than the official (Presbyterian) Church of Scotland. Information on these is provided by Sherry Irvine's article, 'Protestant Nonconformity in Scotland' **www.genuki.org.uk/big/sct/noncon1.html**. A list of Roman Catholic parish registers held by 'Scottish Catholic Archives' can be found at **www.catholic-heritage.net/sca/ genealogy-pr.htm**.

The census in Scotland was taken in the same way as in England. The original returns for 1841, 1851, 1861, 1871, 1891 and 1901, together with indexes, are available on 'Scotlands People'. For 1881, a fully indexed transcript is available, rather than the original returns (although the latter will be added in due course). This transcript may also be viewed at **www.familysearch.org**.

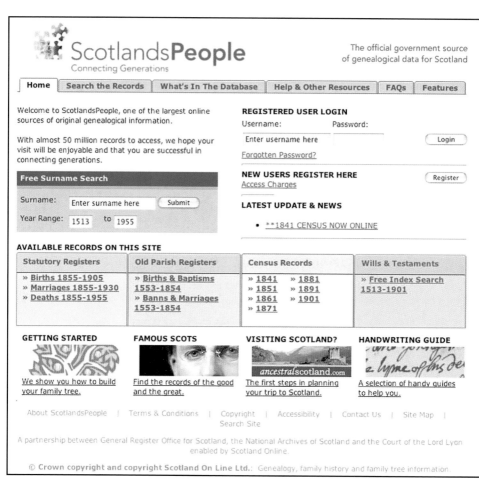

Plate 17. The Scotland People website **www.scotlandspeople.gov.uk** has the basic data needed to trace Scottish ancestors into the nineteenth century and (perhaps) earlier.

Probate records are the fourth major source available on the 'Scotlands People' website. Wills set out the testator's instructions for the disposal of his estate after death, and named the executor. The testament was the formal document created by the court proving the will. Inventories listed the goods of the deceased. Until 1823, wills were proved in ecclesiastical commissary courts; thereafter, in Sheriffs' courts. 'Scotlands

People' has digitised images of over 611,000 probate documents held by the National Archives of Scotland.

Some of the documents available from 'Scotlands People' are also available on other sites. 'FreeCen Scotland' **www.freewebs.com/mmjeffery/index.htm** aims to provide a free to view online census database. Much work still has to be done, but over one-third of the 1841 census is now available. Its sister organization, 'Free REG' **www.freereg.org.uk** is indexing the old parish registers. Work is in progress on eleven Scottish counties. The 'UKBMD' site **www.ukbmd.org.uk** links to many sites containing indexes and transcripts of registration and census information. The 'Scotland BDM Exchange' **www.sctbdm.com** indexes certificates which have been purchased by its contributors. Nearly 45,000 records are listed.

A wide variety of other sources are also available. The 'Scots Find' databases **www.scotsfind.org**, for example, include registers of Edinburgh apprentices and burgesses, various church records such as the *Presbyterie Booke of Kirkcaldie,* marriage registers and indexes to registers and testaments.

The Friends of the Archives of Dumfries & Galloway currently provide nine different databases on their 'Historical Indexes' page **www.dumgal.gov.uk/historicalindexes**. These include various kirk session and burgh records, shipping registers, jail books, and Poor Board minutes.

Another important database is provided by the *'Scotsman* Digital Archive' **archive.scotsman.com**. This has digitised images of the *Scotsman* newspaper from 1817 to 1950. Coverage will be extended in due course. Searching is free, but consultation of an article requires payment of a subscription. Some public libraries have taken out subscriptions, which you may be able to use. Mention has already been made of the *Edinburgh Gazette*, which has been digitised for the twentieth century, and which publishes official announcements on a wide range of matters, e.g. bankruptcy, official appointments, certain regulated professions (e.g. medical personell).

The Scottish Archive Network has a smaller database of '1852-1857 Highlands and Islands Emigration Society Passenger Lists' **www.scan.org.uk/researchrtools/ emigration.htm**.

Much information and advice on sources is available on the websites of major institutions. The National Archives of Scotland has a series of 'Guides' **www.nas.gov.uk/guides/ default.asp** as listed in the box. It also has a variety of guides to the documents in its archives.

The Scottish Archive Network's 'Knowledge Base' **www.scan.org.uk/researchrtools** (click on 'Knowledge Base') provides many similar guides. This site's 'Family History' section has a number of pages on 'My ancestor was . . .' They cover policemen, paupers, land- owners, students, and a number of other occupations.

National Archives of Scotland guides

- Adoption
- Buildings
- Court of Session (1) - Introduction to processes
- Court of Session (2) - Unextracted processes
- Court of Session (3) - Extracted processes
- Court of Session (4) - Other series
- Court of Session (5) - Sequestrations
- Crafts and trades
- Crime and criminals
- Customs and Excise
- Deeds
- Divorce
- Education
- Emigration
- Estate Records

- High Court Criminal Trials
- Inheriting Lands and Buildings
- Lighthouses
- Military Records
- Published Record Sources
- Records of the Poor
- Sasines
- Soldiers & Airmen's Wills
- Taxation Records
- Valuation Rolls
- Wills and Testaments

Scottish Archives Network Knowledge Base guides
- Censuses & Quasi-Censuses
- Death & Burial Records
- Liquor Licensing Registers
- Passenger Lists
- Passports
- Photographs
- Poor Relief Registers
- Postal Directories
- Sasine Abridgements
- School Admission Registers
- Valuation Rolls
- Vehicle Registers
- Wills & Testaments

'Scottish Handwriting.com' **www.scottishhandwriting.com** is a separate site established by the Scottish Archive Network. It offers an online tutorial for those who want to develop their palaeographical skills. This is likely to be a useful site if you wish to consult the wills offered by 'Scotlands People'.

The problems of identifying places were discussed in chapter 7. For Scotland, the 'Gazetteer for Scotland' **www.geo.ed.ac.uk/scotgaz** is very detailed, It includes current and historic general information on each place mentioned, with extracts from historic and contemporary maps. A 'Gazetteer of Scottish Places' can also be found at **www.scan.org.uk/researchrtools**. There are two important collections of digitised maps. The 'National Library of Scotland' **www.nls.uk/digitallibrary/map/index.html** has digitised thousands of maps in its collection, including Ordnance Survey town plans. 'Charting the Nation' **www.chartingthenation.lib.ed.ac.uk** also has over 3,500 historic maps of Scotland.

Numerous other Scottish sites can be found via 'Genuki' pages **www.genuki.org.uk/big/sct**. A full listing is provided in *Scottish Family History on the Web,* which serves as a companion volume for this chapter.

Further Reading

RAYMOND, STUART A. *Scottish family history on the web.* 2nd ed. F.F.H.S., 2005.

STEWART, ALAN. *Gathering the clans: tracing Scottish ancestry on the internet.* Phillimore, 2004.

---

12. Wales

The Principality of Wales was formally united with England in 1536. Historically, it was governed from Westminster. Its records are similar to those of England. Central government records are mostly held by 'The National Archives' **www.nationalarchives.gov.uk**. Local government records are held by county record offices. These are listed by the 'Archives & Records Council Wales' at **www.llgc.org.uk/cac**. There is also a separate listing of 'Welsh Record Offices and Archives on the Web' **www.oz.net/~markhow/welshros.htm**. The 'Archives Network Wales' **www.archivesnetworkwales. info** provides a listing of the collections held by Welsh record offices.

Many Welsh records may be found in the 'National Library of Wales' **www.llgc.org.uk**, which also houses a large collection of books related to Wales. Catalogues of both its book and manuscript collections are available online.

Records of the Court of Great Sessions (the Welsh equivalent of Assizes) are in the National Library. The `Crime and Punishment' database, based on its records can be searched at **www.llgc.org.uk/sesiwn_fawr/index_s.htm**. Some 500 parish registers are held. Details of deposited 'Church in Wales records' are at **www.llgc.org.uk/index.php?id=485**. In addition to parish registers, these include bishops' transcripts, marriage bonds, and various other diocesan records. This page includes a searchable database of marriage bonds, pre-1838.

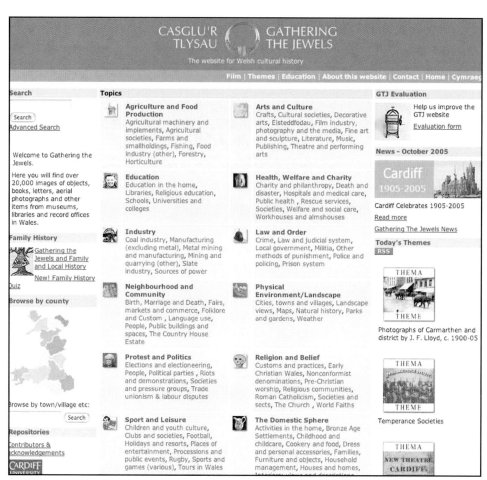

Plate 18. Gathering the Jewels **www.gtj.org.uk** has digitised many of the records in the National Library of Wales, including much of interest to family historians.

Many documents held by the National Library have been digitised. 'Gathering the Jewels' **www.gtj.org.uk** has about 20,000 digitised images, including a few parish registers. The 'Digital Mirror' **www.llgc.org.uk/index.php?id=122** also has many digitised images, including the 'St.Asaph notitiae' which lists heads of households in St.Asaph diocese in the late seventeenth century.

Much general information about Wales may be found on Genuki's 'Wales' pages **www.genuki.org.uk/big/wal/index.html**. The 'Wales Research Outline' at **www.familysearch.org** (click on 'search' and 'research helps') also provides useful guidance.

Aid in locating Welsh places is provided by the 'National Gazetteer for Wales' **homepage.ntlworld.com/geogdata/ngw/home.htm**. Its place-name index includes the Ordnance Survey grid reference, the historic county, alternative versions of the name, and the various present day administrative areas. Samuel Lewis's *Topographical dictionary of Wales* (1844), which provides brief historical accounts of each place listed, is available by subscription at **content.ancestry.com/iexec/?htx=List&dbid=8616**.

13. Offshore Islands

The Isle of Man and the Channel Islands are crown dependencies with their own governments. Censuses for these islands were taken at the same date as the British census, and the returns are available as discussed in chapter 4. However, the system of civil registration was quite different: in Jersey it began in 1842, but in Sark not until 1915. No civil registration indexes for any of the islands are currently available online.

'Genuki' **user.itl.net/~glen/genukici.html** has pages for all the Channel islands, including separate pages for Guernsey, Jersey, Alderney, and Sark - each of which has its own government. 'Alex Glendinning's Channel Islands Pages' **users.itl.net/~glen/CIintro.html** offers much helpful advice and many links, as does Frances Coakley's 'Manx Note Book' **www.isle-of-man.com/manxnotebook**. The latter includes extracts from most Manx parish registers. John Fuller's 'Channel Islands Genealogy' **www.rootsweb.com/~jfuller/ci.html** includes a mailing list, a surname interests list, a list of volunteers willing to look up information for you, and some links to other sites.

On the Channel Islands, the 'Priaulx Library' **www.priaulx.gov.gg** is the main library for Guernsey. It holds civil and parish registers. For Jersey, the 'Société Jersiaise' has an 'Introduction to Family History Research' **www.societe-jersiaise.org/_pages/_family_history.html**.

The Manx National Heritage Library's webpage has a page on 'Sources for Family History' **www.gov.im/mnh/heritage/library/publicinfo/familyhistory.xml**. The library holds the island's civil, parish, and some nonconformist registers, together with a variety of other sources.

Index